HOCKEY LEGENDS
of All Time

Morgan Hughes

Consultant: Joseph Romain

PUBLICATIONS INTERNATIONAL, LTD.

Morgan Hughes is the former editor of *Hockey Stars* and *Hockey Heroes* and has written about hockey for such national publications as *Goal*, *Hockey Scene*, and *Inside Sports*. He co-authored the *Hockey Almanac* and served as consultant for *Great Book of Hockey*. A freelance writer, he has also contributed to *The Sporting News*, *Village Voice*, and *Sport*.

Joseph Romain is the former librarian and associate curator of the Hockey Hall of Fame and Museum in Toronto. He is a freelance writer and library consultant who has written several hockey books, including *The Pictorial History of Hockey* and *Hockey Hall of Fame*. He served as consultant for the *20th Century Hockey Chronicle*.

Louis Weber, C.E.O.
Publications International, Ltd.
7373 North Cicero Avenue
Lincolnwood, Illinois 60646

Manufactured in U.S.A.

8 7 6 5 4 3 2 1

ISBN: 0-7853-1689-2

Library of Congress Catalog Card Number: 95-72995

Contents

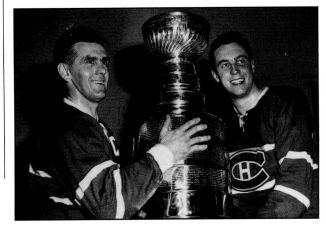

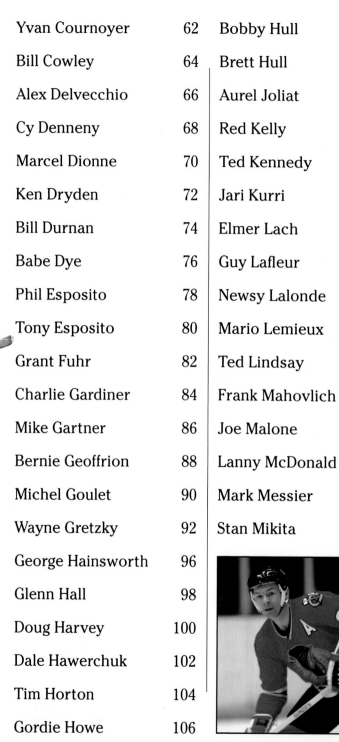

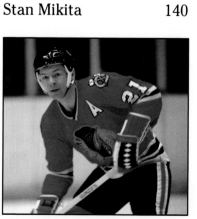

Introduction

Two key elements have contributed to the success of hockey during much of the last century. First, there is the game itself. Characterized by tremendous speed and elegance, hockey is punctuated by the constant thump and crash of high-velocity, shoulder-to-shoulder collisions. It is this characteristic—along with the unrivaled beauty and grace of the action and the heavy price paid for each goal—that has attracted fans to the game for decades. The very nature of the world's fastest sport, its multifaceted brilliance, makes it thrilling to watch.

Second, and just as important, are the men who have made it so exciting. By strapping on pads and lacing up skates, these players bravely crossed over the line from the realm of spectators to the often dangerous domain of armed gladiators.

Detroit's "Production Line" of Gordie Howe, Sid Abel, and Ted Lindsay won four league titles.

"Rocket" Richard played 18 seasons with Montreal, earning eight Stanley Cup rings.

The list of heroes whose accomplishments would make them worthy of inclusion in *Hockey Legends* is long and packed with tales of honor and glory. The 100 players selected for this edition, however, have set themselves above all others. Among them are the greatest scorers of all time (namely, Wayne Gretzky and Gordie Howe), as well as the most intense and ferocious NHLers the game has ever seen—men like Maurice "Rocket" Richard, Bobby Clarke, and Eddie Shore.

These champions, who defined the game of hockey with their skill and determination, still inspire respect and admiration. *Hockey Legends* spans the decades, taking a look at the great offensive stars (from Jean Beliveau to Bobby Hull, Phil Esposito, and Marcel Dionne), the outstanding defensemen (like Raymond Bourque, Doug Harvey, and

Top: Three legends in action—Tony Esposito (in goal), Bobby Hull, and Phil Esposito. *Left*: Pittsburgh ace scorer Mario Lemieux.

Larry Robinson), and the most gifted goalies (such as Glenn Hall, Georges Vezina, Jacques Plante, and George Hainsworth).

What makes these men legendary? It isn't just a numbers game. Not only were these competitors notable for their stats, but also for the style, the grace, and the grit that they brought to the sport. Consider Gretzky's amazing feat of scoring 50 goals in 39 games, shattering a 37-year-old league record held by Maurice Richard (whose 50 goals in 50 games was long considered untouchable).

While Richard was a physical force, Gretzky's style was pure finesse. And then there's Gretzky's idol, Gordie Howe—a great scorer in his own right and an awesome fighter when challenged. Howe played professionally into his 50s, making a dramatic comeback to play on a forward line with his two sons, Mark and Marty, in the late 1970s.

And don't forget those goalies, many of whom played in the pre-mask era. Try to put into context Glenn Hall's amazing streak of 502 consecutive starts without missing a call. Then turn your attention to Terry Sawchuk's unparalleled 103 career shutouts in 971 games.

The history of hockey is filled with tales of both triumph and heartbreak. Bobby Orr, the brilliant defenseman of the Boston Bruins in the early '70s, revolutionized the way the defense position was played with his puckhandling skills. But his career was tragically cut short by knee injuries that might not have proven so destructive had they occurred today. Who knows how great Orr's achievements might have been had he played longer. Chuck Gardiner was at the height of his pucktopping career when he died of a brain tumor—at the age of 30. And Mario Lemieux bravely battled crippling back injuries as well as Hodgkin's disease to become a superstar in the NHL.

All of these players, whether scoring champions or puckstoppers, have in common the fact that during their wonderful careers they stood head and shoulders above their compatriots. They excelled in a difficult and demanding game, where split-second reactions make the difference between winning and losing, between scoring a goal or making a save, between success and failure.

Hockey Legends is filled with the personalities that have made hockey the greatest game in the world, the stories that make up this wonderful history, and the colorful images of a game that continues to capture the imagination of ever-increasing numbers of fans across North America.

Wayne Gretzky (left) led the Oilers to four Stanley Cup triumphs; Denis Potvin (right) captained the Islanders to four consecutive Cup wins.

Sid Abel

In 1948–49, the Detroit Red Wings were heavily favored to win the Stanley Cup. Their top scoring line featured Sid Abel, a brilliant playmaker and goal-scorer, at center, with a pair of talented, hard-nosed wingers—Ted Lindsay and Gordie Howe—on either side. The Wings soared to a regular season title, winning 34 games and leading the NHL in goals. Abel, the heart and soul of Detroit's offensive arsenal, banged home 28 goals, tops in the league. For his splendid effort, he was selected as the league's most valuable player, winning the Hart Trophy for the only time in his 14-year career.

Unfortunately for the Red Wings, who'd last won the Stanley Cup in 1942–43, nobody told the Toronto Maple Leafs that Detroit was destined for another title. In the 1949 playoffs, the Wings barely eked out a seven-game series win over Montreal in the opening round before falling to the Leafs in four straight in the finals. Abel was disabled by Toronto, held without a point in the championship round.

The Wings bounced back in 1949–50, and Abel scored a career-high 34 goals. The "Production Line" of Abel, Lindsay, and Howe combined for 92 goals and 215 points. In the playoff finals against New York, the Wings survived double overtime in Game Seven to win their fourth Stanley Cup.

Sidney Gerald Abel (born February 2, 1918) was a teen playing hockey in Saskatchewan when a Detroit scout spotted him and introduced him to Red Wings manager Jack Adams. After finishing his pre-NHL apprenticeship with the Flin Flon Bombers in 1937, Abel signed with Detroit and spent a year in the minors, skating in Pittsburgh and scoring well (45 points). He made his NHL debut in 1938–39 and quickly impressed everyone with his great determination and grit. Though small by NHL standards, he played a fearless, full-speed style during every shift of every game.

Teamed with Lindsay and Howe, Abel helped the Red Wings win three Stanley Cups (1943, 1950, and 1953). After scoring 189 goals and 472 points in 613 career games, he retired in 1953–54, but later returned to the Wings as a coach. Though he never again tasted Stanley Cup championship champagne, he earned high marks as one of the greatest players in that organization's marvelous history. He was voted to the Hall of Fame in 1969. His number 12 jersey was retired last year, joining those of Terry Sawchuk (1), Larry Aurie (6), Lindsay (7), Howe (9), and Alex Delvecchio (10), hanging from the rafters of Joe Louis Arena.

Abel was an All-Star both as center and left wing.

Syl Apps

The Toronto Maple Leafs were down three games to none against Detroit in the 1942 Stanley Cup finals, and hope was all but lost. In Game Four, with the Red Wings leading 3–2 in the third period, Syl Apps, a sleek center with infinite grace and skill, beat goalie Johnny Mowers to tie the score. Then, with just over seven minutes to play, Apps set up Nick Metz's game-winner, and the Leafs began the greatest comeback in NHL history, winning four straight games—the only time a team down 3–0 in the finals came back to win the Cup. Apps finished the playoffs tied with Detroit's Don Grosso for the lead in points (14) and was tops in assists (nine).

Apps arrived on the NHL scene in 1936, a 21-year-old former collegiate athlete who'd made news in three sports—hockey, football, and track. As an NHL rookie he skated with Busher Jackson and Gordie Drillon and led the league in assists (29). Despite his lack of NHL seasoning, he finished second overall in scoring, with 45 points, close behind New York Americans left winger Sweeney Schriner. Apps was the overwhelming choice for the Calder Trophy as rookie of the year.

Charles Joseph Sylvanus Apps (born January 18, 1915) hailed from Ontario and was a bright student who attended McMaster University in Hamilton, where, along with playing hockey, he competed on the track team as a pole vaulter and on the gridiron as a running back. He proudly represented Canada in the 1936 Olympiad as a vaulter before signing with the Maple Leafs prior to the 1936–37 season.

Known for his finesse and adroit mastery of the game's finer points, Apps was the consummate hero to a nation of hockey fans, combining sportsmanship with surgical precision. A slick playmaker, he was both cunning and brave. By no means a belligerent player, he nevertheless demonstrated an ability to defend himself, though he always kept his penalty minutes low. In 1941–42 he won the Lady Byng Trophy for his sportsmanship.

After serving in World War II—and missing two full NHL seasons, (1943–45)—he returned as a war hero and led the Leafs to two more Stanley Cups (1946–48). He finished his 10-year career with 201 goals and 432 points in 423 games—and only 56 penalty minutes!—before entering the Hall of Fame in 1961. His son, Syl Apps, Jr., also enjoyed a successful 10-year NHL career but never reached the greatness of his father, who some consider the greatest finesse player ever to pull on a Leafs sweater.

An exceptional athlete, Apps lived and played like a gentleman.

Ace Bailey

Despite the rough and tumble nature of the game, fewer than half-a-dozen pro hockey players have died as a result of injuries suffered on the rink. Ace Bailey, one of the game's great "little men," very nearly joined the select ranks of NHL fatalities in the 1930s. During a game between his Toronto Maple Leafs and the Boston Bruins just two weeks before Christmas 1933, Bailey ran afoul of Eddie Shore, a reputed and feared tough guy. Shore hit Bailey with a two-hander to the back, launching the small right winger into orbit. Bailey landed on his head and was rushed to the hospital, where he fought for his life and endured two life-saving operations to relieve pressure on his swollen brain.

The NHL's first All-Star Game was played in Bailey's honor in January 1934, and he took that opportunity to shake hands with Shore and officially exonerate the hard-hitting defenseman of any guilt. But the damage was already done.

Tragically, Bailey never played another game.

Irvine Wallace Bailey (born July 3, 1903) played junior hockey in his home province of Ontario before catching the attention of the Leafs, who brought him to the NHL as a

Bailey was the first Maple Leaf to lead the NHL in scoring.

23-year-old rookie in 1926. In 1928–29, just his third pro season, Bailey led the league in goals (22) and points (32), winning the Art Ross Trophy as scoring champ for the only time in his eight-year career.

Bailey followed with seasons of 22 goals in 1929–30 and then a career-high 23 goals in 1930–31 before his produc-

tion began to fall off. In 1931–32, he played on the Leafs' second line while the top line of Busher Jackson (most points), Joe Primeau (most assists), and Charlie Conacher (most goals) dominated the league scoring races.

The Leafs went all the way to the Stanley Cup finals in 1933—the first time in Bailey's tenure. Up two games to none in the best-of-three finals against New York, the Leafs were ahead 4–1 in the third period of Game Three when Bailey scored at 15:07 to increase the lead to 5–1. The Rangers stormed back with three goals, but the Leafs won, 6–4. Bailey's goal, his only one of the finals, counted as the Cup-winner.

Though he was known throughout his 314-game career as a remarkable penalty killer, he also knew how to play with the puck, scoring 111 career goals and 193 points. He also banged and crashed his way to 472 penalty minutes. He was elected to hockey's Hall of Fame in 1975.

Hobey Baker

Though he never played a single game in the NHL, Hobey Baker was—and remains today—one of the most respected men in all of hockey, whether Canadian or American. Every year, the United States college hockey player of the year is awarded with a trophy in Baker's name. Baker is still referred to as "hockey's American immortal," the first truly great hockey player born in the United States.

A respected scholar in the class-room and a gentle-man on the ice, Baker first gained national prominence during his Ivy League career with the Princeton Tigers, where he earned a pair of intercollegiate hockey titles and filled hockey arenas with fans eager to wit-ness his great skill.

Hobart Emory Hare Baker (born January 15, 1892) came from the small town of Wis-sahickon, Pennsylvania. He played amateur hockey in the Northeast and made his way to Princeton University in 1910. He also skated for the St. Nicholas Club in New York City. During a challenge match

A hero of amateur and college hockey, Baker (left) was the first American to shine at Canada's game.

against the Montreal Stars (held in Quebec), he helped his team to a dramatic upset of the heavily favored Canadian squad, raising eyebrows and eliciting many compliments even from the ranks of his adversaries (who couldn't believe—considering his great talent—that Baker wasn't from Canada).

Following his brilliant col-legiate career, he opted to join the United States Air Force rather than turn pro as a hockey player, though it was believed by the over-whelming majority that he would have thrived in the NHL. With World War I raging in Europe, Baker became a distinguished combat pilot, surviving many harrowing missions. On December 21, 1918, he volunteered to test a plane that had been beset by mechanical prob-lems. Thought to be successfully repaired, the plane lost power in flight and crashed. An American hero on many fronts, Baker was dead at just 26 years of age.

The "grandfather" of Amer-ican amateur hockey was posthumously elected to the Hall of Fame in 1945.

Andy Bathgate

Known primarily as a dangerous scorer and a great finesse player, Andy Bathgate was also instrumental in bringing the face mask to all NHL goalies after injuring Jacques (The Snake) Plante with one of his monster slap shots in the late 1950s. For more than a decade, Bathgate was the pride and joy of the New York Rangers, leading them in scoring and in overall class.

Bathgate joined the Rangers in 1952–53, a 20-year-old who would play a marginal role for two years, seeing little ice time. In 1954–55, he earned a regular job with the Rangers, playing 70 games and scoring 20 goals. The next year, he finished second in the NHL in assists (47). In 1958–59, he reached a career high in goals (40) and points (88), finishing third in the NHL in goals, second in assists, and third in points—a performance that earned him the Hart Trophy as the league's most valuable player. In 1961–62, he notched 84 points in 70 games, including a league-high 56 assists,

and shared the NHL scoring title with Blackhawks scoring ace Bobby Hull. The following year he finished second overall in points (81) behind Detroit's Gordie Howe (86). In 1963–64, he led the NHL in assists (58) and was fourth in points (77).

After participating in the attempted formation of the first players' union, he was traded to Toronto during his brilliant 1963–64 season. He sipped Stanley Cup champagne as a member of the Leafs that year. In Game Seven of the finals against Detroit, Bathgate scored at 3:04 of the first period to give Toronto a 1–0 lead. Goalie Johnny Bower held the Red Wings off the scoreboard and Bathgate's goal held up as the Cup-winning goal.

Andrew James Bathgate (born August 28, 1932) left Winnipeg to play junior hockey at Guelph (Ontario) in the late 1940s. He led the Biltmores to the 1951–52 Memorial Cup (Canadian junior hockey's national title) before turning pro with the Rangers. He

played 719 games for the Broadway Blueshirts, ripping 272 goals and 729 points. He later joined Detroit in 1965 after his brief stint with the Maple Leafs, and was a member of the Pittsburgh Penguins' expansion roster in 1967–68. He retired in 1968, but returned in 1970–71 with the Penguins and, at the age of 38, scored 44 points in 76 games. He skated very briefly in the WHA before hanging up the skates for good in 1975. Three years later

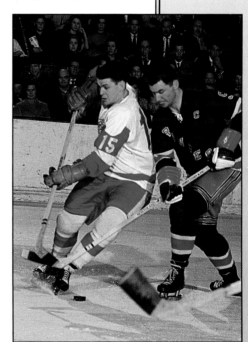

A selfless player, Bathgate twice led the NHL in assists.

he was elected to the Hall of Fame, the fifth all-time leader in assists by a right wing.

Jean Beliveau

On November 5, 1955, Montreal hosted Boston in a regular season game in which history was made—though no record was set.

Jean Beliveau, the Habs' fast-rising superstar, scored on Bruins goalie Terry Sawchuk just 42 seconds into the second period during a two-man power play advantage. Just 26 seconds later, "Les Gros Bill" converted a second pass from linemate Bert Olmstead and beat Sawchuk again. To make the night complete, Beliveau skated in on the ensuing face-off and once more turned an Olmstead relay into a goal,

Beliveau was a part of 10 Stanley Cup-winning Montreal teams.

beating Sawchuk—the winningest goalie in NHL history—for the hat trick, all within 44 seconds! (Amazingly, Beliveau's feat took more than twice as long as the record for the three fastest goals: 21 seconds, by Chicago's Bill Mosienko in 1952.)

Beliveau went on to finish the 1955–56 season with 47 goals and 88 points, leading the NHL in both categories, and earning the Art Ross Trophy as scoring champ and the Hart Trophy as the NHL's most valuable player (the first of two Hart Trophies). On February 11, 1971, in the final weeks of his brilliant 20-year career, Beliveau scored against Minnesota's Gilles Gilbert to become the fourth player in NHL history to reach the 500-goal plateau. Later during that same year, he notched 22 points in 20 playoff games to lead the Habs to their 16th Stanley Cup (and his 10th).

Jean Arthur Beliveau (born August 31, 1931) first gained recognition as a junior player in Victoriaville, Quebec, not far

from his hometown of Trois Rivieres. After a great career with the Citadelles of the Quebec Junior League, where he scored 61 goals and 124 points in 43 games his final year, he became the subject of a bidding war between the Canadiens and the Quebec Aces of the Quebec Senior League, both of whom wanted him for his great size (6'3", 200 pounds) and skill. He chose the Aces and in 1951–52 he scored 45 goals, then added 50 more the following year. Beliveau finally left the Aces for Montreal in 1953–54, and soon was a star in the NHL. A model of consistency, he averaged 1.08 points per game in 1,125 regular season games as well as during 162 playoff games.

A tremendous playoff performer, Beliveau was the original winner of the Conn Smythe Trophy (given to the MVP of the playoffs) when he led the Canadiens to the championship in the spring of 1965. He retired following the 1970–71 season and went into the Hall of Fame in 1972.

Clint Benedict

T hough his name does not generate the same recognition as Georges Vezina, Terry Sawchuk, Jacques Plante, or Glenn Hall, there is no doubt in the minds of hockey historians that Clint Benedict's place in hockey legend is well-earned. It was Benedict's insistence on leaving his feet and dropping to the ice to make saves, despite league rules prohibiting such action, that forced the NHL to rewrite the rule book, permitting "flopping" and forever changing the art of goaltending in the NHL.

Benedict's professional career lasted 18 years (playing in both the NHL and NHA),

In Stanley Cup play, Benedict had an amazing 15 shutouts.

though his NHL career spanned 13 seasons, beginning in Ottawa in 1917. As a member of the Senators, he led the NHL in victories six years in a row (1918–24). He also led the league in goals-against average five years in a row (1918–23) and shutouts seven years in succession (1917–24). He won the Stanley Cup three times as a member of the Senators (1920, 1921, and 1923) before moving to the Montreal Maroons in 1924. He won a fourth Stanley Cup in Montreal in the spring of 1926.

Clinton Stephen Benedict (born September 26, 1894) turned pro with his hometown Ottawa Senators at age 19 when they still were part of the National Hockey Association, prior to joining the NHL. He spent four years in the NHA and was a sturdy, physical goalie known for his ability to take punishment (that is, stitches and broken bones) without missing action. He once donned a leather mask (to protect a broken nose)

that was the precursor to the goalie mask that would come into prevalence many years later, though he ditched it after one game.

After playing 140 of 142 games for Ottawa between 1917 and 1924, he joined the Maroons in 1924–25. He helped Montreal's "other" team to a second-place finish in 1925–26 and won his final Stanley Cup when he stopped Victoria (of the rival Pacific Coast Hockey Association) in a best-of-five final, shutting out the Cougars in Game Four to take the series, three games to one. The very next season, he led the NHL with a 1.51 goals-against average and was runner-up to Canadiens goalie George Hainsworth for the first-ever Vezina Trophy (first awarded in 1926–27).

He retired in 1930 with 190 career wins (among them 57 shutouts). His NHL career goals-against average (2.32) ranks among the best ever—better than Terry Sawchuk's 2.52. Benedict was elected to the Hall of Fame in 1965.

Doug Bentley

By all standards, Doug Bentley was simply too small for the NHL. Standing just 5′8″ and weighing in at 145 pounds, he had the physical stature of a developing teenager, not a professional athlete. But when he joined the Blackhawks in 1939, the left winger quickly proved that he could compete and dominate. In 1942–43, his fourth season with the 'Hawks, he led the NHL in goals (33) and points (73) and won his only Art Ross Trophy as scoring champ.

A great playmaker and finisher, Bentley teamed with his kid brother, Max, who many (including Doug, himself) considered the more talented of the two, and right winger Bill Mosienko to form the famous "Pony Line." Doug was a great stickhandler who could ignite the offense. In 1943–44, while brother Max was fighting in the Canadian army during World War II and missing two seasons of NHL hockey, Doug reached a career high in goals (38), again leading the league in that department. He narrowly

missed capturing his second scoring crown when Boston's Herb Cain (82 points) beat him by five points to take the Art Ross Trophy.

Douglas Wagner Bentley (born September 3, 1916) hailed from Delisle, Saskatchewan, one of 13 kids. At one

A quick and accurate shooter, Bentley was a First-Team All Star three times.

point, four Bentley brothers were playing on the same junior team in Alberta that would send both Doug and Max to the NHL.

Doug missed the 1944–45 season for his own military service, but returned the following season. In 1947–48, the year his brother was traded to Toronto, he led the league with

37 assists. In 1948–49, he was the assists leader (43) and finished with 66 points, just two points behind linemate Roy Conacher for the league scoring title.

Bentley never played for a legitimate Stanley Cup contender. His 'Hawks only made the playoffs five times during his 13-year career and he only went to the finals once. In 1943–44, after trouncing Detroit in five first-round games, Chicago faced Montreal for the Stanley Cup. Habs goalie Bill Durnan held the Blackhawks to eight goals in four games as the Habs swept Chicago in four straight.

Doug and his brother Max were reunited for the 1953–54 season when Rangers boss Frank Boucher talked them into skating for his Blueshirts. Doug came out of retirement for the occasion, and at 37 years of age managed just 12 points in 20 games. He retired in 1954 with 219 goals and 543 points in 566 games and was voted into the Hall of Fame in 1964.

Max Bentley

Max Bentley was a third-year pro with the Chicago Blackhawks in 1942–43, a linemate to his older brother, Doug, and one-third of the NHL's highly respected and feared "Pony Line" when the Rangers came to town for a tilt that would land Max in the record books. In the midst of a shellacking that would send the Rangers home with their tails between their legs, Bentley ripped no fewer than four third-period goals as the 'Hawks ran the score to 10–1 before the final buzzer brought a merciful end to the night. To that point, Max was only the second man in NHL history to achieve such a feat—four goals in one period. Busher Jackson had done it for Toronto in the 1930s.

Max and Doug Bentley (along with Bill Mosienko) gave the Blackhawks most of their offensive power for many years. In 1945–46, after a two-year layoff during which he fought in the Canadian army in World War II, Bentley returned to the NHL and scored 31 goals, led the league in points (61), and was voted the most valuable player, winning both the Art Ross and Hart Trophies. He repeated as scoring champ the following year when he finished the 1946–47 season with a career-high 72 points.

Early in the 1947–48 season, Max became part of a huge blockbuster deal that sent him to Toronto in exchange for five players, including Gus Bodnar, Ernie Dickens, Bob Goldham, Bud Poile, and Gaye Stewart. In Toronto, he helped the Leafs to three Stanley Cup titles (1948, 1949, and 1951).

Maxwell Herbert Lloyd Bentley (born March 1, 1920) came from a large farming family. While he, like his older brother Doug, was very small by NHL standards (just 5'8" and 158 pounds), he was quick as a rabbit and had an uncanny ability to carry the puck through heavy traffic, dipsy-doodling in classic style, and never taking his eye off the developing play. His ability to find his teammates with sharp, accurate passes more than compensated for his lack of size. His outstanding sportsmanship won him the Lady Byng Trophy in 1942–43.

He came out of his retirement in 1953–54 to reunite with brother Doug on a line with the New York Rangers, scoring 14 goals. He retired with 245 goals and 544 points (one more than Doug) in 646 career games—and three Stanley Cup rings. He was voted into the Hall of Fame in 1966.

Toe Blake

Rare is the man who makes a name for himself as a great player and then surpasses his own reputation with greater achievements as a coach. Such a man is Toe Blake, an integral member of Montreal's famous "Punch Line," with Elmer Lach and Maurice Richard in the 1940s. Blake was not only a superb player, winning every major award for his on-ice exploits, but he was also a magnificent coach, leading the Canadiens to eight Stanley Cups—including five straight championships from 1955 to 1960.

Hector Blake (born August 21, 1912) hailed from a mining town in northern Ontario, and came from very poor beginnings. He was discovered playing junior hockey for the Sudbury Wolves, who had captured the 1932 Memorial Cup, and it wasn't long before the aggressive youngster was playing professionally.

Blake joined the Canadiens in 1936 after playing for three seasons with the Montreal Maroons. His rambunctious style earned him respect, and his scoring ability earned him accolades and trophies. In 1938–39, Blake led the NHL in scoring, notching 47 points to win the Art Ross Trophy. He also captured the Hart Trophy as the league's MVP and was dubbed "The Old Lamplighter" for his scoring feats.

In 1943–44, he was united with hard-nosed center Elmer Lach and fire-breathing right winger Rocket Richard, an assignment that would turn the Canadiens into a dynasty. The trio finished the season 1–2–3 in the Habs' scoring race and took the Canadiens to a Stanley Cup, winning eight of nine playoff games. The Blake-Lach-Richard trio accumulated 48 points in those nine games.

In 1944–45, the Punch Line finished 1–2–3 in the league in scoring, as Richard knocked home 50 goals, Lach won the scoring title, and the line accounted for 105 goals and 220 points. On the strength of the Punch Line, the Habs won another Stanley Cup in 1945–46, and Blake, once known for his belligerence, won the Lady Byng Trophy for his sportsmanship.

A shattered ankle ended Blake's playing career midway through the 1947–48 season, and, after bouncing around the minors for several years, he took over as coach of the Habs in 1955–56, leading them to five straight Stanley Cups (1955–60). He added three more titles (1965, 1966, and 1968)

As a player and a coach, Blake embodied excellence in hockey.

before retiring with 13 titles to his credit (as well as 235 goals and 527 points in 578 games). He entered the Hall of Fame in 1966.

Mike Bossy

By 1977–78, when Mike Bossy made his NHL debut, the New York Islanders were no longer a fledgling team fighting for respectability, but rather an up-and-coming team ready to contend for a championship. Bossy arrived with a reputation as a sniper, and quickly established himself as a force. Not only did he run away with the Calder Trophy as the league's top rookie, but he set a new record for goals by a freshman (53). Over the next decade, Bossy carved out a place for himself among the game's all-time leading scorers.

Michael Dean Bossy (born January 22, 1957) was the sixth of 10 children (the fifth of six boys) growing up in Montreal. He was a Quebec junior superstar during his four-year career at Laval, scoring a remarkable 308 goals in 260 games (an average of 1.2 goals per game). The Islanders chose him 15th overall in the 1977 amateur draft and brought him directly to the NHL without a moment's pause in the minors.

Any worries about a sophomore jinx following Bossy's 53-goal rookie year were erased when he ripped a league-high 69 goals in 1978–79 (setting a single-season record for goals by a right wing).

Teamed with center Bryan Trottier and left winger Clark

Bossy was a catalyst for the Islanders' four consecutive Stanley Cup wins.

Gillies, Bossy filled the net year after year, and proved to be a devastating playoff performer as well. In 1980, when the Isles won their first of four consecutive Stanley Cups, he scored 10 goals in 16 games. In 1981, he led all playoff scorers and set a new record (35 points in 18 games). In 1982, he won the Conn Smythe Trophy as playoff MVP when he led all playoff

goal-scorers (17), an achievement he enjoyed yet again in 1983.

Known as much for his non-violent style as for his brilliant scoring, Bossy was public in his disgust for brawling and goons, always turning the other cheek when he became the focus of abuse (which was constant during his 752-game career). He won the Lady Byng Trophy for sportsmanship three times (1983, 1984, and 1986) and was a First-Team All-Star five times. He scored at least 51 goals nine years in a row.

Chronic back injuries forced Bossy to retire after he missed the entire 1987–88 season. At the time of his retirement, he ranked fourth all-time in goals-per-game (.762); third all-time in points-per-game (1.497); third all-time in goals by a right wing (573); second all-time in goals by a rookie (53); first all-time in assists in one season by a right wing (83); and first all-time in points in one season by a right wing (147). He was voted into the Hall of Fame in 1991.

Frank Boucher

No player in the history of the NHL has embodied the properties of sportsmanship and excellence as much as Frank Boucher did during his 14-year NHL career, played almost entirely with the New York Rangers. Boucher won seven Lady Byng Trophies between 1928 and 1935—and when he didn't win (in 1932) he was runner-up to Joe Primeau. His domination of that honor was so great that in 1935 the trophy was officially presented to him to keep, and a new one was cast for future winners.

Boucher was brilliant as a player and magnificent as a coach, winning the Stanley Cup twice in uniform and once

The consummate gentleman, Boucher holds the record for Lady Byng Trophies.

as a rookie NHL coach! Centering the Rangers' top scoring line with Bill and Bun Cook, Boucher was one-third of a line many consider to be among the best ever assembled.

Frank Boucher (born October 7, 1901), one of six hockey-playing brothers, made his NHL debut as a 20-year-old with his hometown Ottawa Senators in 1921, scoring nine goals. He spent the next four years in the Pacific Coast Hockey Association skating for the Vancouver Maroons. When the Rangers came into existence in 1926–27, manager Conn Smythe took a chance on the 135-pound Boucher. Smythe was replaced by Lester Patrick, but Boucher stuck around for the next 12 years. He led the NHL in assists three times and finished among the top five scorers four times.

In 1927–28, as the Rangers won their first Stanley Cup (in just their second NHL season), Boucher was the team's major contributor, scoring seven

goals—including the Cup-winner in Game Five against Canadiens goalie Clint Benedict—and leading all playoff scorers with 10 points. Boucher notched 157 goals and 409 points in 542 games before retiring at the end of the 1937–38 season, with two Stanley Cups to his name. He went immediately into coaching and was an overnight sensation, working his way quickly up the ladder. In 1939–40, Boucher made his NHL coaching debut and led the Rangers to their third Stanley Cup. The Rangers only made the playoffs three more times in the next nine years. Boucher briefly came out of retirement during the 1943–44 season, and scored 14 points in 15 games—at age 42! But he couldn't make the Rangers a winner again.

Known and universally respected for a lifetime of excellence on and off the ice, as well as for his tremendous spirit of sportsmanship, Boucher was voted into the Hall of Fame in 1958.

Raymond Bourque

Only three players have won the James Norris Trophy as the NHL's top defender as many as five times—Bobby Orr (eight), Doug Harvey (seven), and Raymond Bourque (five).

Since he broke into the NHL with the Boston Bruins in 1979–80, Bourque has been one of the most highly respected rearguards in the game. As a 19-year-old rookie, he won the Calder Trophy as the top freshman in the league and steadily built his reputation as the game's premier defender, combining tremendous skill and finesse with hard, clean, physical domination.

Raymond Jean Bourque (born December 28, 1960) was a sensation during three years in the Quebec junior league, playing first at Sorel and then at Verdun, not far from his hometown of Montreal. After scoring 56 goals and 220 points in 204 games, he was the eighth player picked in the 1979 draft. He went directly to the NHL with the Bruins and

notched 65 points in 80 games—then a record for rookie defenders.

In 1983–84, Bourque became only the sixth defenseman in NHL history to reach the 30-goal plateau (31) and was 14th overall in scoring (96 points). In 1984–85, he led the Bruins in scoring for the first time, with 86 points, and earned his fourth First All-Star Team berth. Two years later, in 1986–87, he led the team in scoring again, with 95 points, and earned his first Norris Trophy.

In 1987–88, the Bruins went to the Stanley Cup finals for the first time in a decade. Though they were swept by Edmonton, Bourque tied for seventh in playoff scoring with 21 points in 23 games. Having won his third team scoring title (81 points in 78 games), he was awarded his second straight Norris Trophy.

The Bruins went back to the Stanley Cup finals in 1989–90. That year, against Vancouver, Bourque had the greatest game of his career

In addition to winning five Norris Trophies, Bourque was runner-up for four more.

with a goal and five assists (including his 600th career assist). The Bruins lost to Edmonton again in the finals but Bourque won his third Norris Trophy. He copped the award again in 1991 and 1994.

In 1991–92, he became the third defenseman in NHL history to reach the 1,000-point mark (joining Denis Potvin and Paul Coffey). In 1992–93, he became the second defenseman ever to record 800 assists. As the 1995–96 season began, Bourque needed just 109 points to pass Johnny Bucyk as the Bruins' all-time leading scorer. He stands second on the all-time list in goals, assists, and points by a defenseman.

Johnny Bower

In 1953, at the age of 29, when many players are thinking about packing it in, Johnny Bower was just getting started as an NHL star. In 1968–69, the 45-year-old future Hall of Famer was still stopping pucks with remarkable flair.

Bower made his NHL debut with the New York Rangers in 1953–54 and led the league in minutes (4,200), having stolen the goaltending job from 1952–53 rookie of the year goalie Gump Worsley. But the Rangers didn't hold on to Bower, sending him back to the minors, where he toiled until the Maple Leafs signed him to a deal in 1956–57. The Leafs were a terrible team, having just finished dead last for the first time in their history, and Bower was uncertain of his ability to resurrect them alone.

John William Bower (born November 8, 1924) grew up in Depression-torn Saskatchewan. He served in World War II before finishing his junior eligibility in Prince Albert. Bower turned pro in 1945 with the Cleveland Barons (AHL) and stayed in Cleveland for eight seasons before the Rangers gave him his first break. When Toronto rescued him from minor-league obscurity in 1958, Bower was a 34-year-old "rookie." Still, he breathed new life into the Leafs. Over the next decade, he led them to four Stanley Cup championships.

Bower was tougher than leather, absorbing injuries and untold punishment without the least complaint. It's estimated that he received more than 250 stitches in his face alone during his 552-game NHL career.

In 1960–61, he led the league in wins (33) and goals-against average (2.50) and, at age 37, won the Vezina Trophy. In 1961–62, he helped the Leafs to their first Stanley Cup in 11 years. Though goalmate Al Rollins played the last two games of the finals against Chicago, Bower's 2.20 GA average led all playoff goalies. Bower was in goal the next year when the Leafs successfully defended their title, whip-ping Detroit in five games. He led all playoff goalies with eight wins and a microscopic 1.60 GA average (including a pair of shutouts). The 1964 finals featured Detroit and Toronto in a rematch between Bower and Terry Sawchuk. The series was knotted 3–3 before Bower shut out the Wings in Game Seven to give the Leafs the "three-peat."

Bower shared the goal with ex-rival Sawchuk in 1966–67 when the Leafs won their last Cup, leading the way with a 1.87 playoff GAA. Bower and Sawchuk shared the Vezina Trophy in 1964–65, and among goalies

Bower spent 13 seasons in the minors before starring in the NHL.

with a minimum of 500 career games, he stands tied with Sawchuk for the fourth-best career GAA (2.52). Bower entered the Hall of Fame in 1976.

Frank Brimsek

Hockey nicknames are not gifts. They are hard-earned monikers reflecting respect and achievement. And no man's "handle" more aptly symbolized accomplishment than goalie Frankie Brimsek's. The diminutive goalie from northern Minnesota was known as "Mr. Zero" because of his skill at keeping the puck out of his own net.

As an NHL rookie in 1938–39, Brimsek played 43 games for Boston, leading the league in wins (33), goals-against average (1.56), and shutouts (10). He also took the Bruins to their first Stanley Cup in a decade, winning eight of 12 playoff games and recording a 1.50 GA average. For this tremendous debut, he was awarded both the Calder Trophy as rookie of the year and the Vezina Trophy as the game's top goalie.

Francis Charles Brimsek (born September 26, 1915) was the first U.S.-born player to make a major impact in the NHL. A native of Eveleth, Minnesota, he was a high school star before skating briefly at St. Cloud Teachers College. After failing to make it with Baltimore in the Eastern amateur league, he was on his way home when he landed a job

In his first eight NHL games, Brimsek earned an incredible six shutouts.

with the Pittsburgh Yellow Jackets. In 1937, he signed with the Bruins and spent a year in Providence (AHL), where his chances of usurping netminding giant Tiny Thompson were viewed as remote.

In the fall of 1938, Thompson fell victim to an eye infection. Brimsek's debut was so impressive that the Bruins sold Thompson to Detroit—a vastly unpopular move among Boston fans. But Brimsek, who lost his first game as the Bru-

ins' starting goalie, won his next three without giving up a single goal, playing more than 212 minutes of shutout hockey, approaching Thompson's record of 224 minutes.

Over the next five years, Brimsek won two Vezina Trophies (1939 and 1942) and took the Bruins to a pair of Stanley Cups (1939 and 1941).

Following the 1942–43 season, Brimsek hung up his skates and enlisted in the U.S. Coast Guard, serving two years in the Pacific during World War II. Though he made a courageous return to the NHL in 1945–46, much of the magic was gone. The Bruins were unable to make another run at the Stanley Cup and Brimsek was a shadow of his former self. In 1949 he was sold to Chicago, where he led the league in losses (38) before calling it quits.

In 1966, Brimsek, who shares the fourth-longest unbeaten streak in NHL history (23 games), became the first American to be voted into the Hall of Fame.

Turk Broda

Some players shine most brilliantly when the heat of the spotlight is on them. Turk Broda, who starred for the Toronto Maple Leafs for 14 seasons, was just that kind of player, a "money" goalie whose performances always reached their peak during the most important games. If he was good enough to win a pair of Vezina Trophies for his regular season play, then it was even more characteristic that he led all playoff netminders in goals-against average no less than five times and had a career playoff GAA (1.98) that was significantly lower than his career regular season GAA (2.53).

Broda was known for many things, not only magnificent puck-stopping. He also possessed an indomitable nature that allowed him to laugh in the face of severe challenge and to avoid taking the world or himself too seriously. Once, when Leafs boss Conn Smythe threatened to remove him from the roster if he didn't trim some weight from his abundant 197-pound frame, the goalie (who stood just 5′9″) dieted for a week, made the weight requirement, then went out and shut out the powerful New York Rangers.

Walter "Turk" Broda (born May 15, 1914) was nothing special as a young goalie growing up in Manitoba. He earned his chances in junior hockey due to providence more than accomplishment and in 1936, at the age of 22, he signed with the Leafs and led the NHL in wins (22) as a rookie.

Broda won his first Vezina Trophy in 1940–41 when he led the league in wins (28) and goals-against average (2.06). But he assured his place in history when he took the 1941–42 Leafs to their first Stanley Cup in 10 years. In 1943 Broda left the NHL to serve in WWII. Back in nets full-time by 1946–47, he chalked up 31 victories and won another Stanley Cup. Never one to rest on his laurels, Broda delivered again the following year, winning his second Vezina Trophy with a league-high 32 wins and a 2.38 GAA in the regular season, and a brilliant 8–1 record and 2.15 GAA in the playoffs as the Leafs won a second straight Cup. Broda recorded a minuscule 1.57 GA average in the 1948–49 playoffs as Toronto took a third consecutive Stanley Cup title. The portly netminder with the perpetual smile won his fifth, and final, Stanley Cup in 1950–51 before quitting in 1951–52. Broda went into the Hall of Fame in 1967.

Broda ranks 10th all-time in goalie victories (302).

Johnny Bucyk

In the late 1960s and early 1970s, when the "Big Bad Bruins" dominated the NHL with bruising physical play and intimidation, one of their most vital players, Johnny Bucyk, was banging home goals and winning the Lady Byng Trophy for his good sportsmanship. At six feet and 215 pounds, Bucyk was plenty strong and tough, but his non-belligerent style was almost anomalous in the Boston scheme. In his 23-year career he was known as the ultimate corner man, the winger who did the dirty work along the boards and got the puck to his center.

In 1970–71, his 16th season in the NHL, Bucyk broke out of that role and set personal career-high marks in goals (51), assists (65), and points (116). That year, he won the first of his two Lady Byng Trophies after sitting out just eight minutes in penalties! His 65 assists broke the single-season record for left wingers.

John Paul Bucyk (born May 12, 1935) played junior hockey with his hometown Edmonton Oil Kings in the early 1950s. He was scouted and signed by Detroit and made his NHL debut with one goal in 38 games for the Red Wings in 1955–56. Following his sophomore year, he was traded to Boston for Terry Sawchuk. In Beantown, he was united with Bronco Horvath and Vic Stasiuk, comprising what became known as the "Uke Line," for the players' Ukrainian lineage. With Bucyk feeding him the puck, Horvath finished among the league leaders in goals and points on a regular basis, though the team fell into second-division status.

In 1967–68, the Bruins began a resurgence—with the help of Bobby Orr, Phil Esposito, Wayne Cashman, Ken Hodge, Derek Sanderson, and Gerry Cheevers in goal. They climbed from the cellar into third place, then up to second place the following season. In 1969–70, the Bruins scaled to heights they hadn't enjoyed in nearly three decades, bashing their way through the playoffs and squashing the St. Louis Blues in the finals, four games to none. Bucyk's 19 playoff points were third best after Espo (27) and Orr (20). Upset in the first round of 1970–71

Bucyk holds Bruin records for games, goals, and points.

playoffs, the Bruins bounced back in 1971–72 and won their second Cup in three years. Bucyk's nine goals tied for the playoff lead, and he was third in playoff points (20).

Bucyk retired in 1978, first all-time in assists (813) and points (1,369) by a left wing. He was also second all-time in goals by a left wing (556). He entered the Hall of Fame in 1981.

Gerry Cheevers

The 1971–72 season was the pinnacle of a great career for a superb goaltender from St. Catherines, Ontario, named Gerry "Cheesie" Cheevers. While his Boston teammates on the front lines dominated the opposition physically and on the scoreboard, Cheevers was a veritable brick wall in goal. During one stretch of that memorable campaign—which ended with a Stanley Cup victory against the Bruins' hated rivals, the New York Rangers—Cheevers was undefeated in 32 consecutive starts, setting a league record that may never be broken. Cheevers won 24 games and tied eight in that span, and helped the Bruins to a first-place regular season finish. Ironically, he did not win the Vezina Trophy that year (or any other, for that matter), losing out to Chicago's Tony Esposito.

Gerald Michael Cheevers (born December 2, 1940) grew up across Lake Ontario from Toronto. At 16, he left St. Catherines to attend St.

Michael's College in Toronto, whose Junior A hockey team was sponsored by the Maple Leafs. In 1959–60, he became the first-string goalie for the St. Michael's Majors and was the league's top goalie. Over the next several years, Cheevers, property of the Maple Leafs, bounced around the minors, until Boston drafted him in 1965. He got his big break in 1967–68, when the Bruins protected him in the expansion draft and made him one of their two No. 1 goalies (along with Eddie Johnston).

Cheevers immediately set about establishing his reputation as a fierce competitor, playing with determination bordering on hostility (twice he led all goalies in penalty minutes, with 59 PIM in 1976–77, and 62 PIM in 1979–80). A steady performer all season, he regularly elevated his game to peak levels during the most important showdowns.

After taking the Bruins to two Stanley Cups in three years (1970 and 1972), he

jumped to the World Hockey Association's Cleveland Crusaders, where he led the offense-oriented league in goals-against average in 1972–73 with a 2.84 mark. After three and a half seasons in Cleveland, Cheevers returned to Beantown in 1976, and finished his career with the Bruins. Although Boston reached the finals in 1977 and 1978, he never tasted Stanley Cup champagne again.

Among goalies with 350 NHL games to their credit, Cheevers stands 20th all-time with a 2.89 career goals-against average. He retired in 1980, after nearly two decades of pro hockey, and was immediately named coach of the Bruins, compiling a record of 204–126–46. Cheevers was elected to the Hall of Fame in 1985.

Cheevers holds the NHL record for the longest unbeaten streak by a goalie (32).

Dino Ciccarelli

When you look up "perseverance" in the dictionary, there's no picture next to the definition but there should be. And the picture should be of Dino Ciccarelli. Not only is it amazing that Dino ever made it to the NHL, it's nothing short of remarkable that he's among the game's all-time elite, with more than 500 goals and 1,000 points.

During his second year of junior hockey at London, Ontario, the scrappy right winger suffered a badly broken leg that knocked him out for the season and eliminated him from the ranks of draft-eligible prospects. NHL teams who'd been watching him looked elsewhere. Even when he made a stunning recovery and scored 50 goals and 103 points the next season, he remained virtually ignored. Only the North Stars had faith enough in Dino to sign him as a free agent. In his first full NHL season (1981–82), he paid huge dividends with 55 goals and 106 points.

Dino Ciccarelli (born February 8, 1960) hails from Sarnia, Ontario, and was a junior sensation long before he entered the NHL, tearing a 72-goal hole in the broadside of OHL goaltending as a member of the London Knights at age 17.

He scored 50 goals and surpassed the 100-point mark twice during his nine-year stint in Minnesota before being traded to Washington in 1989. After three solid years with the Capitals (112 goals and 209 points in 223 games) he was all but given away to the Red Wings for Kevin Miller. Ciccarelli proved he still had it by scoring 41 goals during his first year in Detroit (1992–93).

Ciccarelli scored 16 hat tricks with Minnesota—tops for the team.

He added 28 more the following year despite injuries that limited him to just 66 games.

There's nothing fancy about Ciccarelli. He's the ultimate warrior, a player who does most of his damage from in-close and who frequently absorbs savage beatings from bigger, stronger defensemen, but never backs away from an encounter, especially if the puck is still up for grabs.

On January 8, 1994, during a 6–3 blowout of the Kings in Los Angeles, Dino fired a shot past Kelly Hrudey for his 500th career goal, becoming the 19th player in league history to reach that estimable plateau. After an injury-plagued 1994–95 season in which he scored 16 goals and 43 points in 42 games, he went to the Stanley Cup finals for the second time in his career (he did it with the 1980–81 North Stars as a rookie). Though heavily favored to win the Stanley Cup, his Red Wings were swept by New Jersey and Ciccarelli suffered the ultimate disappointment.

King Clancy

The legend of King Clancy was established in 1923, during his third pro season with Ottawa, when the Senators were battling Edmonton for the Stanley Cup. In the finale of the challenge series, the Senators, having earlier eliminated Vancouver, held a precarious 1–0 lead against the Eskimos on Punch Broadbent's first-period goal. With injuries decimating the Ottawa lineup, Clancy, a man of great talent and enthusiasm, stepped in and played every position—including goal when Clint Benedict was whistled to the penalty box.

Clancy spent a total of nine years with the Senators, winning a pair of Stanley Cups, before he was traded to Toronto in the midst of the Depression when financial straits were crippling the Ottawa franchise. Maple Leaf owner Conn Smythe (who had won the money for Clancy from betting on a horse) took a huge gamble—and it payed off. Clancy was a huge sensation in Toronto, helping the Leafs win the 1932 Stanley Cup. Because of his appeal and drawing power, Maple Leaf Gardens is still known as "the house that Clancy built."

Francis Michael Clancy (born February 25, 1903) was raised in Ottawa, where he was an accomplished athlete in several sports despite the fact that he did not boast a very formidable physique. When he first tried out for the Senators at age 18, he stood just 5'9" and weighed in at an almost unbelievable 125 pounds. He later grew into a more respectable frame—and though he was small, he demonstrated great courage and never backed away from any player.

Known for his exuberant nature, Clancy was also respected as a quick-footed skater whose choppy stride got him around the rink with great haste if not the utmost grace. In 1928–29, Clancy was the NHL's top goal-scoring defender when he registered 13 tallies. In 1929–30, he led all NHL defensemen in scoring when he recorded a career-high 17 goals and 40 points. He was traded to Toronto the very next year and notched 21 points—third overall among backliners behind Boston's Eddie Shore (31) and George Owen (25). Clancy led all defensemen in goals again in 1932–33 when he scored 13 times.

Clancy was a colorful character both on and off the ice.

After playing 592 games over 16 NHL seasons, Clancy retired in 1936, coached the Montreal Maroons for half of the 1937–38 season, and then became an NHL referee. As a testament to his great reputation, he was actually a popular official—a rarity in any era. He later coached the Leafs. In 1958 he was elected to the Hall of Fame and in 1988, the King Clancy Memorial Trophy for humanitarian work was established in his honor.

Bobby Clarke

During the championship heyday of the Philadelphia Flyers in the mid-1970s, no player better symbolized the win-at-any-cost attitude of the Broad Street Bullies than their captain, Bobby Clarke. A brave and tireless warrior, Clarke was a lethal scoring threat (twice leading the NHL in assists) and a brilliant checker, winning the Frank Selke Trophy in 1982–83 as the league's best defensive forward.

Much of Clarke's finest play came during the 1974 and 1975 playoffs, when the Flyers became the first expansion team to win the Stanley Cup. While he did not lead his team in scoring, he was the inspirational fulcrum of the Flyers' effort.

Robert Earle Clarke (born August 13, 1949) was a junior hockey star in his hometown of Flin Flon, Manitoba, where he played so well his jersey was retired when he ended his tenure with the Bombers, a tribute paid to precious few juniors. Despite a diabetic con-

dition that required daily insulin injections, Clarke became the 17th player chosen in the 1969 draft, and he beat long odds to make the Flyers in 1969–70, finishing his rookie NHL season with 15 goals and 46 points.

Clarke was the first expansion team player to record a 100-point season.

Over the next 13 years, he established his reputation as one of the league's most talented and determined centers. He blasted 35 goals as a third-year pro in 1971–72 and won the Masterton Trophy for perseverance and dedication. In 1972–73, he notched his first 100-point season, finishing with 37 goals and 104 points, and was voted the NHL's most valuable player. In 1973–74, Clarke finished fifth in league

scoring and led the Flyers to a thrilling six-game Stanley Cup final victory over the powerful Bruins. As a "command performance" of sorts, Clarke sparkled in 1974–75, leading the NHL in assists (89), earning his second Hart Trophy as league MVP, and spearheading the Flyers' successful defense of their Stanley Cup title.

While the Flyers' mini-dynasty ended with a four-game sweep at the hands of the Montreal Canadiens in the 1976 Stanley Cup finals, Clarke continued to reign among the game's top centers. He led the league in assists yet again in 1975–76 and recorded a career-high 119 points, enough to garner his third MVP award.

Clarke retired in 1984 with 358 goals and 1,210 points in 1,144 career games covering 15 seasons—along with a pair of Stanley Cup rings. He spent six years as Flyers GM before holding the same post for one year in Minnesota. In 1994 he returned to Philly as president and GM. Clarke was voted into the Hall of Fame in 1987.

Sprague Cleghorn

Superstar or disgrace—which of these labels best characterized Sprague Cleghorn? Arguments can easily be made on either side. A man of unbridled vigor and aggressiveness, he was known to knock opponents out of games with his hard-hitting belligerence, but also to play a solid, talented game of hockey, anchoring the defense and helping several teams win Stanley Cup championships.

In the early days of organized professional hockey, during the first two decades of the 20th century, Cleghorn played in New York, Montreal, and Ontario prior to the official inauguration of the NHL in 1917. A good skater who'd rush with the puck and barrel through the opposition, Cleghorn scored 16 goals in 1919–20—an impressive total for a defenseman in that era.

After helping the Senators to a pair of Stanley Cup championships in 1920 and 1921, he was obtained by Montreal, a deal that made Cleghorn very bitter toward his former

employers. In a game during the 1921–22 season, he went on a personal rampage, conducting assaults on ex-teammates Eddie Gerard, Frank Nighbor, and Cy Denneny—the cream of the Senators roster—knocking them out of the game. As a result, Ottawa police stepped in and had to be persuaded not to arrest Cleghorn. (A decade earlier, while skating for the Montreal Wanderers, Cleghorn had narrowly averted incarceration when he opened a nasty gash on the head of Newsy Lalonde—then playing for the Habs—with a crosscheck.) The rambunctious defender made no apologies for his actions, which were labeled as "a disgrace" by the official in charge of the game, and went on to finish the season with a career-high 17 goals—second best among NHL defenders after Toronto's Harry Cameron (19).

Sprague Cleghorn (born in 1890) was destined to play for his hometown Habs. Though he spent many of his early years traveling from team to

team, league to league, he eventually made his way home and played his greatest hockey with immortal teammates such as Howie Morenz, Aurel Joliat, and Georges Vezina—as well as his own brother, Odie, who spent seven seasons with the Habs.

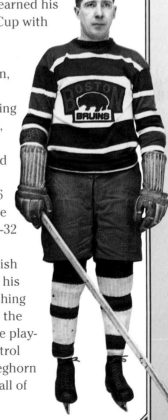

Cleghorn earned his third Stanley Cup with Montreal in 1923–24, then went to Boston, where he finished his playing career in 1928, with 84 goals, 123 points, and 489 penalty minutes in 256 NHL games. He took the 1931–32 Maroons to a third-place finish before ending his one-year coaching career. One of the most fearsome players ever to patrol NHL rinks, Cleghorn entered the Hall of Fame in 1958.

Paul Coffey

Experts insist that the key to Detroit's outstanding regular season and subsequent charge to the Stanley Cup finals in 1994–95 was the presence of Paul Coffey. Not only because Coffey is a four-time Stanley Cup champion—three times with Edmonton and once with Pittsburgh—but because Coffey, an unchallenged team leader, had embraced the philosophy of the coaching staff and had, by his unassailable example, shown his teammates what was required to be a true winner. Of course, it didn't hurt that Coffey had one of his more brilliant years, leading all league defensemen in scoring with 58 points in 45 games despite his age (34) and years of NHL service (15).

Though his Red Wings were ultimately swept from the finals by New Jersey, Coffey earned the consolation of winning his third Norris Trophy (his first two came back-to-back in 1985 and 1986 while he was in Edmonton). At the start of the 1995–96 season, Coffey was the all-time leader among NHL defensemen in goals (358), assists (978), and points (1,336). Only three players in NHL history (Wayne Gretzky, Gordie Howe, and Marcel Dionne) have more assists than Coffey.

Paul Douglas Coffey (born June 1, 1961) played his junior hockey at Sault Ste. Marie and

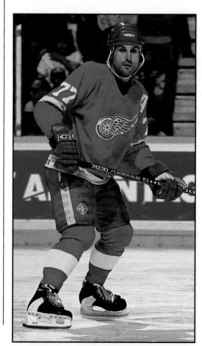
Coffey is the all-time NHL scoring leader among defensemen.

Kitchener in the Ontario league, where he caught the eye of NHL scouts. In 1980, he was Edmonton's first selection in the draft (sixth overall), and he turned pro immediately. After a tentative 32-point rookie year in 1980–81, Coffey exploded with seasons of 89, 96, 126, 121, and 138 points over the next five years. During that span, he won his first two Norris Trophies and also put his name to Stanley Cup championships in 1984 and 1985. On March 14, 1986, he entered the record books with an eight-point game (including six assists) against Detroit, joining only 11 others.

After winning his third Stanley Cup in 1987, Coffey refused to report back to the Oilers following a contract dispute with GM Glen Sather. After a lengthy holdout, he was traded to Pittsburgh, where he teamed with Mario Lemieux to forge a championship team in 1991. Traded to Los Angeles in 1992, his stay in a Kings jersey was relatively short as Detroit acquired his services in 1993.

Charlie Conacher

In the 1980s, there was Mike Bossy; in the 1970s, Guy Lafleur; in the 1950s and 1960s, Gordie Howe; and in the 1940s, Maurice "Rocket" Richard. All were dominating right wingers whose shot was feared by goalies and whose competitiveness was the object of admiration. In the early 1930s, Toronto Maple Leafs right winger Charlie Conacher, known respectfully as "The Bomber," was the cream of the NHL's crop of starboard snipers, if a some-what less rounded player than his brother Lionel.

From 1930–31 through 1935–36, Conacher led the league in goals five times. In 1931–32, he scored 34 times (capturing his second goal-scoring title) and was the vital "finisher" on the fabled "Kid Line," with Joe Primeau and Busher Jackson. In the 1932 playoffs, he shared the goal-scoring lead (six) with Ranger winger Bun Cook as the Leafs swept New York in three games to win their first Stanley Cup in 10 years.

Charles William Conacher (born December 10, 1910) hailed from Toronto and was the ultimate hometown hero. He played for the legendary Marlies of the Ontario Junior A league before signing with the Maple Leafs in 1929. He scored in his first game, against Chicago, and never looked back, finishing his rookie season with 20 goals.

One of the game's first "power forwards" (before that phrase became a cliche), Conacher used his size and physical strength to command his space on the ice. In 1933–34, as a fifth-year pro, he won his first scoring title when he led the league in goals for the third time in four years (32) and points (52). He reached career highs the following year (1934–35) when he led the NHL in goals (36) and points (57).

The Leafs never won another Stanley Cup during Conacher's nine-year hitch, and he missed much of the 1936–37 and 1937–38 seasons because of injury, playing only 34 games of a possible 96. As Toronto fell on hard times in the late 1930s, Conacher was traded to Detroit. In 1938–39, he scored just eight goals in 40 games, and was traded to the New York Americans, where he spent the last two years of his NHL career (1939–41).

Big, strong, and fast, Conacher led the NHL in goals five times.

From 1947 to 1950, Conacher had an undistin-guished career as coach of the Chicago Blackhawks, a strug-gling team whose most pro-ductive player was his own brother, Roy (who won a scor-ing championship of his own in 1948–49). Charlie Conacher quit coaching just a year before his son, Pete, made it to the NHL with the Blackhawks. The Bomber went into the Hall of Fame in 1961.

Alex Connell

Among NHL goalies with a minimum of 350 games to their credit, Connell shares the lowest all-time career goals-against average, a startling 1.91. Connell's arch rival, George Hainsworth (who played 465 career games to Connell's 417), also finished his outstanding career with a 1.91 GAA.

Connell managed a stretch of shutout hockey during the 1927–28 season, for Ottawa, that landed him in the record books. Earning six straight shutouts—an unprecedented accomplishment—he surrendered not a single goal over a span of 461 minutes and 29 seconds.

Connell—the "Ottawa Fireman"— was the ultimate clutch goalie.

Though he finished the season with a 1.30 GA average, he was second best to Hainsworth of the Canadiens.

Alex Connell (born in 1902) was raised in Ottawa, where he was a great hockey star as well as a skilled baseball and lacrosse aficionado. He signed with Ottawa in 1924 and was forced into the uncomfortable assignment of replacing legend Clint Benedict, who'd taken the Senators to three Stanley Cups before his trade to Montreal.

Connell didn't waste much time winning over Ottawa fans. In his second NHL season (1925–26), he led the league in victories (24) and goals-against average (1.17). In 1926–27, he won 30 games, tops in the NHL, and took his Senators (who were powered by Frank Nighbor and Cy Denneny) to the Stanley Cup finals against the Bruins. In four games against Boston, Connell allowed only three goals as Ottawa won the series with two victories and two ties. Connell's playoff GA average was an unbelievable 0.67 in six games.

Following his brilliant shutout performance in 1927–28, Connell's team began a downward slide that ended with a last-place finish in 1930–31, during which the star goalie led the league in losses (22). Financial trouble spelled doom for the Senators and prior to the 1931–32 season, Connell, Hec Kilrea, and several others went to the Detroit Falcons (later renamed the Red Wings). Connell played only one season for Jack Adams' Falcons before bouncing back to Ottawa in 1932–33, then on to the New York Americans before finally landing in Montreal, where he took the Maroons to a Stanley Cup title in 1934–35, sweeping Toronto (with rival Hainsworth in goal) in the finals. Connell, a three-time runner-up for the Vezina Trophy, retired in 1937 tied with Tiny Thompson for fifth all-time with 81 career shutouts among his 199 victories. He went into the Hall of Fame in 1958.

Bill Cook

Frank Boucher, unarguably one of the greatest players in the history of the New York Rangers franchise, once said that Bill Cook, a rugged farmer from western Canada, was the best player ever to wear a Rangers jersey.

In the 1928 Stanley Cup finals, Cook, just a second-year pro, assisted Boucher's Cup-winning goal against Clint Benedict and the Montreal Maroons in Game Five, giving the Rangers their first-ever NHL championship.

Cook was a highly skilled, intense competitor, who was in many ways the forerunner to the Gordie Howe style of play, combining tremendous grit with talent in an awe-inspiring mix. Though he didn't make his NHL debut until he was 30 years old, Cook immediately established his credentials by winning the 1926–27 Art Ross Trophy as the league's scoring champ, with 33 goals and 37 points.

William Osser Cook (born October 9, 1896) arrived in Brantford, Ontario, 65 years before the town's next most famous son, Wayne Gretzky, was born. Despite his great hockey skill as a youngster, Cook gave up the chance to turn pro in his 20s, instead

Tough as a soldier, "Bad Bill" Cook used his stick like a marksman.

answering the call to serve in World War I. He returned to Canada and began farming in western Canada, but soon joined up with Saskatoon of the Western Hockey League. When the Rangers were assembled in 1926, Cook was one of the first players signed by Conn Smythe.

In no time, the line of Bill Cook, Frank Boucher, and Cook's kid brother, Bun, was dominating the NHL. Bill, the line's right winger, was tough and stern, a perfect complement to the grace and elegance of his center, Boucher.

In 1931–32, Cook reached a career high in goals (34), tying Toronto's Charlie Conacher for the league lead, and finished fifth overall in points. The following year, Cook won his second scoring title with 28 goals and 50 points. His finest moment came in the 1933 playoffs. In the finals, against Toronto, the Rangers took a two-games-to-one lead into Game Four, which turned into an epic goaltenders' battle between Rangers netminder Andy Aitkinhead and former Ranger Lorne Chabot. Into scoreless overtime, Cook took a pass from Butch Keeling and fired past Chabot to give the Rangers the Cup.

Cook retired in 1937, with 229 goals and 367 points in 452 NHL games. He was elected to the Hall of Fame in 1952.

Yvan Cournoyer

During his 16-year NHL career, Yvan Cournoyer's Montreal Canadiens made 15 trips to the Stanley Cup playoffs. Ten of those quests resulted in championships—a 66.7 percent success rate! No other team in NHL history has enjoyed such an amazing achievement.

Cournoyer, a speedy right winger, was the most valuable player in the 1973 playoffs and a major contributor to each of those Stanley Cup winners, spending much of his career on a line with Hall of Fame center Jacques Lemaire. In 1973, when the Habs needed just 17 games to win three best-of-seven series, Cournoyer notched 25 points—among them 15 goals—to lead all post-season scorers in goals and points. The pinnacle of his superb playoff exhibition came when he blasted the Cup-winning goal—his sixth of the finals alone—against Chicago goalie Tony Esposito midway through the third period of Game Six, giving the Habs a 6–4 victory and their 17th title.

Yvan Serge Cournoyer, known as the "Roadrunner" (born November 22, 1943), was raised in Quebec, where he played junior hockey in Montreal prior to making it to the NHL as a 20-year-old in 1963, though he played only briefly. In 1964–65, his official rookie season, the Roadrunner scored seven goals in 55 games, but in subsequent seasons his goal totals rose to 18, 25, 28, and 43. Cournoyer suffered a slump in 1969–70, scoring just 27 goals, but he bounced back the next year with 37, then reached a career-high 47 goals in 1971–72, play-ing with Lemaire and Frank Mahovlich.

Standing just 5'7", Cournoyer compensated for a lack of sheer physical presence with tremendous speed. He was a darting skater with great acceleration and a laser beam for a shot. Shooting left-handed off the right wing—just as Rocket Richard had done before him—gave Cournoyer an increased shooting angle, and he took great advantage of this edge to score 428 career goals in 968 NHL games (plus 64 more in 147 playoff contests).

Though he never led the NHL in goals, earned a scoring title, or won a major regular season award, Cournoyer was one of the most dangerous weapons in the Canadiens' arsenal. Until he was usurped on the right wing by a young superstar named Guy Lafleur in the early 1970s, Cournoyer was the Habs' chief sniper. He retired following the 1978–79 season with 863 points, and was elected to the Hall of Fame in 1982.

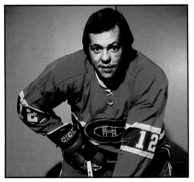
Cournoyer played on 10 Stanley Cup-winning Habs teams.

Bill Cowley

The Boston Bruins would never have won the 1939 Stanley Cup were it not for Bill Cowley. In fact, without their slick second-line center, they never would have made it into the final round at all. Many would credit Mel "Sudden Death" Hill with moving the B's past the Rangers in the semifinals—it was he, after all, who scored no less than three overtime goals (Games One, Two, and Seven). But Cowley was the crafty playmaker who fed three perfect passes to Hill (a mediocre regular season scorer) after his first choice, Roy Conacher, was checked into submission.

By the time the Bruins hoisted the Stanley Cup after defeating Toronto in five games, Cowley emerged as the playoffs' leading scorer with 11 assists and 14 points in 12 games, including the assist on Conacher's Cup-clincher in Game Five.

William Mailes Cowley (born June 12, 1912) was raised in Quebec and, surprisingly, didn't start playing hockey until he was 12 years old. He was playing with the Ottawa Shamrocks in 1934 when he was discovered and signed to an NHL contract. He played for the St. Louis Eagles in 1934–35, but they folded under financial pressure and Cowley moved to the Bruins, where he spent the next dozen years.

Somewhat overshadowed by the dazzling "Kraut Line" of Woody Dumart, Milt Schmidt, and Bobby Bauer, Cowley nevertheless made his presence felt on the Bruins. In 1940–41, he notched 62 points—tops in the league—to win the Art Ross Trophy. That year he was also voted the game's most valuable player, winning the first of his two Hart Trophies. He was voted the game's MVP again in 1942–43, when he led the league in assists (45) and finished just one point behind scoring champion Doug Bentley of the Chicago Blackhawks, who won the Art Ross Trophy with 73 points to Cowley's 72.

The clever playmaker led the league in assists three times during his career and was a member of two Stanley Cup champions (1939 and 1941). He finished his career with 548 points in 549 games— a mark of his consistency and productivity—and a reputation for hard, clean play. He was a

Cowley was the unsung hero of the Bruins in the late 1930s and early '40s.

remarkable playoff performer, as his display in the 1939 playoffs demonstrated, remaining cool and calculating under the most high-pressure circumstances. Cowley was elected into the Hall of Fame in 1968, a full 20 years after hanging up his skates.

Alex Delvecchio

Only one man in the history of the league has played more NHL games than Alex "Fats" Delvecchio, the round-faced centerman who crafted a Hall of Fame career pivoting a line with Gordie Howe, the all-time leader in games played.

During a 24-year NHL career playing entirely with the Detroit Red Wings—another remarkable feat—Delvecchio filled the skates previously worn by Sid Abel (Howe's original center), and established his own reputation with solid production and unflappable good sportsmanship.

Delvecchio was just 19 when the Red Wings brought him to Detroit for a one-game "cup of coffee" during the 1950–51 season. By the following year, he was ready to make his official debut, which featured 15 goals and 37 points in 65 games. In 1958–59, his eighth full season in the NHL, Delvecchio notched 54 points while sitting out just six minutes in penalties, an accom-

plishment that earned him the first of his three Lady Byng Trophies. He grabbed his second in 1965–66, with 69 points and 16 PIM, and his third in 1968–69, when he reached a career-high 83 points (includ-

Delvecchio is tied with Tim Horton for second all-time in seasons played (24).

ing the leagues' fourth-best assists total, 58) while serving just four minor penalties for eight minutes.

Alexander Peter Delvecchio (born December 4, 1931) first caught the eye of Detroit scouts while playing junior hockey in his home province of Ontario, where his graceful skating and precision passing made him a very promising future property. He signed

with the Red Wings while still a teenager and broke into the league to stay at the beginning of the 1951–52 season.

His rookie year, spent as a third-line center behind Abel and Glen Skov, ended with a Stanley Cup ring. By the 1952–53 season, he had moved up to the top line with Howe and Ted Lindsay, and he finished second in the league in assists (43) behind scoring champ Howe (who led the NHL in goals, assists, and points). The Wings won two more Stanley Cups in the next three years (1954 and 1955).

At the start of the 1962–63 season, Delvecchio was named captain of the Wings, an honor he held for 10 years. He retired from active duty (after playing just 11 games in the 1973–74 season) with 1,281 points in 1,549 career games. He coached and managed the Red Wings briefly during the mid-1970s and went into the Hall of Fame in 1977. His number 10 jersey, which hangs in Joe Louis Arena, is one of only six retired by the Red Wings.

Cy Denneny

Near the end of the 1920–21 season, second-place Ottawa was tangling with fourth-place Hamilton in a meaningless game. Left winger Cy Denneny, the Senators' leading scorer, was busy chasing down Montreal's Newsy Lalonde for the league scoring title with the season drawing to a close. During this March 21 game against Hamilton Tigers goalie Howie Lockhart, Denneny made up considerable ground, ripping six goals as his team declawed the Tigers, 12–5. (Earlier that year, Cy's big brother Corbett, playing for first-place Toronto, had also scored six goals against Lockhart. Talk about sibling rivalry!) Denneny finished the year with 34 goals (one behind league leader Babe Dye of the Toronto St. Pats) and 39 points (two shy of Lalonde).

One of the greatest goal-scoring threats of all-time, Denneny still holds the third-best goals-per-game average of all-time, at .767 (behind Mario Lemieux, .825, and Brett Hull, .797).

Cyril Denneny (born in 1897) first skated professionally with the Toronto Shamrocks of the NHA in 1915, at just 18. When the Shamrocks folded, the Denneny brothers joined the Toronto Arenas, where Cy played one season before being traded to Ottawa, where he had his greatest years.

During the 1917–18 season (the league's inaugural campaign), Denneny—a 20-year-old, first-year NHLer—scored a career-high 36 goals in 22 games (assists were not yet being recorded), second only to Montreal's Joe Malone (44). The Senators finished third in the four-team league. The following year, Ottawa won the regular season title on the scoring of Denneny and Frank Nighbor (18 goals each) and the netminding of Clint Benedict, who led the league in both wins and goals-against average.

In 1919–20 the Senators won their first Stanley Cup, taking the regular season title in a runaway, then sneaking

past Seattle (PCHL) in the Cup challenge. Oddly, Denneny was held without a point. In 1920–21, the Senators dropped to second place, but earned a Stanley Cup finals berth against Vancouver, ousting the Millionaires in five games.

Denneny won the Art Ross Trophy as NHL scoring champ for the only time in 1923–24 (22 goals, 23 points). After helping the Senators to their fourth Stanley Cup in 1927, he moved to Boston and, despite a marked decline in production, shared in the Bruins' first-ever Cup title in 1928–29. He retired following the 1929 playoffs with 246 goals in 326 regular season games. After far outshining his big brother over a 12-year NHL career, Cy Denneny entered the Hall of Fame in 1959.

Denneny's accurate shooting skills made up for his lack of speed on the ice.

Marcel Dionne

Small, fast, and smart—and gifted with tremendous skill—Marcel Dionne proved in the 1970s and 1980s, when the game was becoming dominated by bigger, tougher players, that a small man not only could compete but could prosper. By the time he concluded his 18-year NHL career, Dionne was third all-time in goals, assists, and points. Only one other center (Wayne Gretzky) has more assists.

On December 14, 1982, skating for the Los Angeles Kings, Dionne scored the 500th goal of his career, a feat previously accomplished by only eight other men in NHL history. He then proceeded to add 231 more goals to that total before retiring.

Marcel Elphege Dionne (born August 3, 1951) hailed from Drummondville, Quebec. A brilliant junior player during two seasons with the St. Catherines Blackhawks of the Ontario league, he led the OHA in scoring (55 goals and 132 points) as a rookie in 1969–70, then followed up with a second scoring title the next year (143 points). The Detroit Red Wings picked him second overall in the 1971 draft after Dionne led his junior team to a league playoff title.

Dionne was an instant NHL smash, scoring 28 goals as a rookie in 1971–72, then 40 as a sophomore. He spent four years in Motown, where despite his great scoring (139 goals, 366 points in 309 games) the crafty center was unhappy, and the team was a loser. In 1975–76, he signed with the Kings as a free agent. During the next eight years he notched six 50-goal seasons (53, 59, 53, 58, 50, and 56) and won the Art Ross Trophy with 137 points, a career high, in 1979–80.

Though he was overshadowed in the yearly scoring races by the likes of Guy Lafleur (Montreal), Brian Trottier (Islanders), and Gretzky

Dionne was the driving force behind the Kings' "Triple Crown" line.

(Edmonton), Dionne was rewarded for his outstanding play and great sportsmanship with a pair of Lady Byng Trophies (1975 and 1977) and was runner-up for two more. He also was a runner-up for the Hart Trophy as MVP in 1980. He received his greatest—and most deserved—honor when he won two straight Lester B. Pearson Awards (1979 and 1980), as the players' choice for the NHL's most valuable player.

Following his 1987 trade to the Rangers, Dionne's career finished in 1988–89 with 731 goals 1,771 points in 1,348 games (1.3 points per game). It was Dionne's curse never to play on a Stanley Cup contender. (His kid brother, Gilbert, won a Cup with Montreal in 1993.) One of the greatest natural talents ever to play the game, Dionne entered the Hall of Fame in 1992.

Ken Dryden

No one will ever accuse Montreal Canadiens goalie Ken Dryden of staying at the party too long. His brilliant career began with a sensational rookie performance in the 1971 playoffs and ended with a sixth Stanley Cup in eight tries in 1979. Before you could catch your breath, the heady goaltender with the law degree and the analytical mind called it quits at just 31, with only eight years of NHL service under his belt—retiring for the second time in his all-too-short career.

Dryden was a lanky figure in goal, standing 6'4" and weighing in just over 200 pounds. Known for leaning upright on the knob of his goalstick during breaks to ease the ache in his back, he

Dryden won five Vezina Trophies in his brief, but remarkable career.

was a quick-witted puck-stopper who could outthink—and therefore outguess—the majority of NHL shooters.

In 1970–71 Dryden, a recent graduate of Cornell University (where he played his college hockey while studying), played just six games for the Canadiens. But he stepped in during the 1971 playoffs, playing all 20 games as the Habs won the Cup. Tony Esposito, Ed Giacomin, and Bernie Parent had better goals-against averages, but Dryden posted the 12 victories necessary to take the title.

Kenneth Wayne Dryden (born August 8, 1947) traveled from his hometown of Hamilton, Ontario, to attend Cornell and then McGill Law School on his way to the NHL, a journey that also detoured briefly in the AHL.

In 1971–72, with a Conn Smythe Trophy as playoff MVP to his credit, he began his official NHL rookie year and led the league in wins (39), which earned him the Calder Trophy as rookie of the year. He won

his first Vezina Trophy the following season, when he won 33 games and led the league with a 2.26 GA average.

Dryden shocked the hockey world when he announced, following the Canadiens' 1973 Stanley Cup victory, that he was taking the 1973–74 year off to work as a clerk in a Toronto law firm. The Habs struggled during his hiatus, so they inked him to a new, more lucrative deal in 1974–75.

Dryden only once lost as many as 10 games in a single season—the 1975–76 campaign—and that year he recorded a career-high 42 wins and won his second of five Vezina Trophies with a 2.03 GA average (his lowest ever). He won 80 of 112 playoff games in eight years and 258 of 397 regular season contests. He retired with six Stanley Cup rings and a career GA of 2.24 (2.40 in playoff action). Author of several insightful hockey books, Dryden entered the Hall of Fame in 1983, at the ripe old age of 36.

Bill Durnan

Considered by many the greatest goalie in the history of the NHL, Bill Durnan, who had a short but storied pro career, has often been compared to fellow Canadiens netminder Ken Dryden, who followed in Durnan's footsteps some 20 years after Durnan retired. One major difference: Dryden broke in with the Habs at age 23 while Durnan didn't play in the NHL until he was 27, late in life for a "rookie."

Durnan's NHL career spanned just seven seasons, for a total of 383 games. In 1943–44, as a freshman, he led the league in victories (38) and goals-against average (2.18) and became the second rookie to win the Vezina Trophy, an award he would earn six times (1943–47 and 1948–50).

William Ronald Durnan (born January 22, 1916) seemed destined to play for his hometown Toronto Maple Leafs. Growing up in the shadows of Maple Leafs Gardens, he skated in the Leafs' farm system and earned a reputation as a promising future star, partic-ularly after backstopping the Sudbury Wolves of the Ontario junior league to a Memorial Cup championship in 1931–32. Injured in the off-season, he was suddenly abandoned by the Leafs and briefly quit

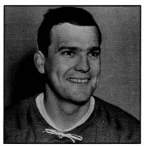

Durnan earned the prized Vezina Trophy six out of his seven years in the NHL.

hockey. In 1940, he took the goalie job with the Montreal Royals of the Quebec senior league and quickly caught the eye of Canadiens scouts with his ambidextrous style. Three years later, after much hesitation, he agreed to sign a pro contract with the Habs, making his debut in 1943–44.

During his first four NHL seasons, he led the league in wins (38, 38, 24, and 34) and goals-against average (2.18, 2.42, 2.60, and 2.30) and helped the Habs win a pair of Stanley Cups (1944 and 1946). Durnan also earned a rare distinction when he was named captain for the Canadiens, an honor seldom given to goalies.

If Durnan was brilliant in the regular season, he seemed even more invincible during playoffs, where he twice finished with GA averages under 2.00. In his rookie year, he posted an amazing 1.53 playoff average; in 1946–47, when the Canadiens lost in six games to Toronto in the finals, Durnan surrendered just 22 goals in 11 games, finishing with a 1.97 GA average in a losing cause.

During the 1948–49 season, he set a modern record for shutout hockey when he slammed the door on shooters for 309:21, the fourth-longest shutout streak in NHL history. Citing nervous anxiety, Durnan cut his career short in 1950. Among goalies with at least 350 games, he ranks ninth all-time in career GA (2.36). He was elected to the Hall of Fame in 1964.

Babe Dye

One of the early superstars of the NHL, Babe Dye starred for the Toronto St. Pats during the 1920s, when the league was brand new. Dye was a powerful shooter with a knack for scoring "big" goals—goals that not only helped his team win but also effectively demoralized the opposition.

Cecil Henry Dye (born May 13, 1898) grew up in Hamilton, Ontario, the product of a single-parent household (his father died when he was just a toddler). Dye's mother was determined to give him the same chances all the other boys had. He played for the Hillcrest Seniors (of the Ontario senior league) before helping De La Salle win a title in 1917. He served in World War I and then returned to hockey in 1919, signing up with the St. Pats.

In 1920–21, as a second-year NHLer, the 22-year-old Dye led the league with 35 goals in 24 games, finishing third in total points behind Montreal's Newsy Lalonde and Ottawa's Cy Denneny. The fol-lowing year, he led all playoff scorers with nine goals and 10 points as the St. Pats won the Stanley Cup with a five-game series victory over the power-ful Seattle Millionaires of the PCHL. In Game Five, Dye scored four goals, including the Cup-clincher early in the first period as the St. Pats rolled to a 5–1 win to take the series.

In 1922–23, Dye won his first Art Ross Trophy when he led the NHL in goals (26) and points (37), but the St. Pats' defense was suspect, and they fell to third place in the stand-ings. Two years later, Dye cap-

A distinguished athlete, Dye was once offered a baseball contract by the Philadelphia Athletics.

tured his second scoring title when he blasted a career-high 38 goals and 44 points in just 29 games—a remarkable 1.3 goals per game.

In 1926–27, he went to the Chicago Blackhawks, where he played on a line with Dick Irvin and Mickey MacKay. Dye ripped 25 goals—tying Howie Morenz for second in the league—and his line accounted for 57 of the Black-hawks' league-high 115 total goals, but the team couldn't get past Boston in the first round of playoffs.

Disaster struck the follow-ing fall when Dye suffered a broken leg during training camp prior to the 1927–28 sea-son. He ultimately played only 11 games and recorded not a single point. He bounced back with the New York Americans in 1928–29, but scored just once in 42 games before calling it quits. He came out of retire-ment briefly in 1930–31 with Toronto, but it didn't last. Dye finished with 202 goals in 271 NHL games, and was inducted into the Hall of Fame in 1970.

Phil Esposito

His critics called him the ultimate "garbage man" because he banged home a great majority of his 717 career goals from the slot area 15 feet in front of the enemy goal, but Phil Esposito was a strong-wristed goal-scoring machine who was the fulcrum of the Big Bad Bruins of the 1970s, a multiple scoring champion, and the fourth all-time leading goal-scorer in the history of the game.

In 1970–71, Esposito set a modern-day record when he ripped 76 goals in 78 games. Though he would be eclipsed by many subsequent scoring aces, Espo charted new territory and earned himself a place in the history books.

Philip Anthony Esposito (born February 20, 1942) grew up in Sault Ste. Marie, Ontario, and began to hone his shooting skills early in life, victimizing his little brother, Tony, who later became a Hall of Fame goalie in the NHL. Espo was a hulking teen who failed to impress Junior A coaches in Ontario until he was 19 and caught on with the St. Catherines Blackhawks, a subsidiary of the NHL Blackhawks. He scored 32 goals and 71 points in 49 games and earned a pro contract, though he would spend most of the next two years in the minors. In 1964–65, he made the NHL for good, centering a line with Bobby Hull and Chico Maki and notching 55 points. Two years later, Espo was traded to the Bruins—a deal the Hawks would sorely regret.

In 1967–68, Esposito led the NHL in assists (49), and the next year he won his first scoring championship, with 126 points (his league-high 77 assists set an NHL record). The Bruins became a dominant team in 1969–70 with Espo on the front line (leading all goal-scorers with 43) and Bobby Orr on defense (winning the scoring title with 120 points). The Bruins won the Stanley Cup in 1970 as Espo ripped 13 goals and 27 points in 14 playoff games. The Bruins won another Cup in 1972, thrashing the Rangers in the finals as Espo and Orr each notched 24 points.

Espo eventually won five scoring titles and twice was named the NHL's most valuable player to go with his pair of Stanley Cup rings. During the 1975–76 season, he was traded to the arch-rival Rangers—a deal that stunned him. Still, he took New York to the brink of a Stanley Cup in 1979 before losing to Montreal in the finals. He retired during the 1980–81 season and later became GM of the Rangers and Tampa Bay. Ranked fourth all-time in goals and points, and fifth in assists, Esposito was voted into the Hall of Fame in 1984.

Tony Esposito

In 1968–69, the Chicago Blackhawks finished dead last in the Eastern Division, despite the league-leading 58-goal performance of Bobby Hull. Just one year later, in 1969–70, those same Blackhawks finished first in the Eastern Division, due largely to the outstanding rookie goaltending of Tony Esposito, who led the NHL in wins (38), goals-against average (2.17), and shutouts (15). For this brilliant showing, Esposito won both the Calder Trophy as rookie of the year as well as the Vezina Trophy as the game's top goalie, making him just the second player—the first since Frank Brimsek in 1939—to accomplish the Calder-Vezina double-dip.

Anthony James Esposito (born April 23, 1943) grew up in the Ontario port town of Sault Ste. Marie, brother to one of the NHL's most accomplished goal-scorers, Phil Esposito. The two enjoyed healthy competition as kids, with older brother Phil shooting against younger brother Tony, each honing the skills that would one day make them superstars in the NHL. In his teens, instead of playing Junior A hockey, Tony accepted a scholarship to the Michigan Institute of Technology, where he earned a degree in business administration. After graduation in 1967, he signed with the Montreal Canadiens and played minor pro hockey in Vancouver and Houston before getting his NHL break in 1968–69 (a 5–3–4 record in 13 games). The Habs left him unprotected in the 1969 draft, and Chicago grabbed him, installing him as the No. 1 goalie. As a rookie, Esposito proved he belonged.

A pure reflex goalie, "Tony O" came to be known as the chief proponent of the "butterfly" style of goaltending. Rather than playing a "stand-up" version, he would crouch with his feet out, his knees together in an inverted V shape, leaving a gaping "five hole" between the pads that he would quickly slam shut if shooters were foolhardy enough to fall for the trap.

In 16 years of NHL competition, Esposito climbed to the very upper echelons of goaltending greatness, finishing third all-time in games played (886), third all-time in career wins (423), and seventh all-time in career shutouts (76). Among the elite handful of NHL goalies with more than 800 games to his credit, Esposito ranks sixth in career goals-against average (2.92). Tony O never won a Stanley Cup in Chicago, losing twice to Montreal in the finals (1971 and 1973), but his consistent play and reliability made him a superstar. He was voted into the Hall of Fame in 1988.

Though his style was unorthodox, Esposito was a three-time First-Team All Star.

Grant Fuhr

During the years of Edmonton's reign of terror in the mid-1980s, Oiler goalie Grant Fuhr was to the defensive side of the puck what Wayne Gretzky and Mark Messier were to the offensive side. He was the brick wall, the last outpost, the "money" goalie who won the big games with miraculous saves. Fuhr wasn't just lucky to be part of those great teams, he was one of the reasons they were great.

During the 1981–82 season, when the Oilers were still climbing the ladder, trying unsuccessfully to knock the Islanders off the top of the mountain, Fuhr demonstrated his magic with a 23-game undefeated streak that included 15 victories and eight ties. While he fell short of Gerry Cheevers' record 32-game undefeated streak, Fuhr proved he was more than a scarecrow in goalie garb. He was a bona fide star.

Grant Fuhr (born September 28, 1962) grew up in western Canada and began his junior career at 17 with the Victoria (B.C.) Cougars. He was the league's top rookie in 1979–80, winning 30 of 43 games. In 1980–81, he led the WHL in shutouts and was voted the WHL's top goalie. The Oilers picked him eighth overall in the first round of the 1981 draft and installed him in nets in 1981–82, giving him 48 rookie starts. He went 28–5–14 as a freshman.

Fuhr won his first Stanley Cup in 1983–84, sharing goaltending duties with Andy Moog. He then carried almost the entire load the following year, when the Oilers repeated as playoff champs, winning 15 of 18 starts in the 1985 post-season. After winning his third Stanley Cup in 1986–87, he enjoyed his most dominant year in the NHL in 1987–88, setting an NHL record with 75 appearances in goal. He led the league with 40 victories and was rewarded for his outstanding play with his only Vezina Trophy.

By the time the Oilers won their fifth Stanley Cup in 1989–90, Fuhr had fallen from grace with Edmonton management and was placed as a backup to Bill Ranford. Traded to Toronto prior to the 1991–92 season, he then moved to Buffalo midway through the 1992–93 season, where he battled injuries and Dominik Hasek for playing

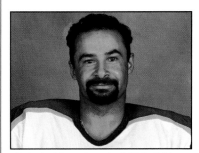

Fuhr's 14 assists in 1983–84 is a single-season goaltender record.

time. The Los Angeles Kings acquired him during the 1994–95 season, but he was unable to get them into the playoffs.

Fuhr's resume is the stuff of Hall of Famers. Just 10 wins shy of 300 for his career as the 1994–95 season concluded, he still has those five Stanley Cup rings, that Vezina Trophy, and a reputation as one of the great money goalies of all time.

Charlie Gardiner

Smiling Charlie Gardiner, who dominated the NHL with his superb goaltending during an all-too-short seven-year career, came into the league with great promise and went out in a flash of ultimate glory. On April 10, 1934, with his Chicago Blackhawks in a tense battle of survival against Detroit in the Stanley Cup finals, Gardiner, terminally ill (though unaware of his own condition), battled pain and extreme fatigue to hold the Red Wings scoreless through four-and-a-half periods of hockey, including 30 minutes of sudden-death overtime. In the finale of his great career, he held the fort until Mush March could find a chink in the Detroit defense and score the goal that won the 1934 Cup—the first in Chicago's history.

Two months later, despite surgery designed to save his life, Gardiner was dead from complications caused by an untreated case of uremia, originally thought to have been brought on by an infection in his tonsils.

Charles Robert Gardiner (born December 31, 1904) moved from Edinburgh, Scotland, to Winnipeg, Manitoba, at the age of seven. He was playing for the Winnipeg Maroons in 1926 when he was discovered by the brand new Chicago Blackhawks. After Hugh Lehman took the 'Hawks through their inaugural season, Gardiner was brought in for the 1927–28 campaign, during which Chicago finished last and Gardiner led the league in losses (32).

As a sophomore, Gardiner lost a league-high 29 games despite a 1.93 goals-against average as the 'Hawks won just seven games. In 1929–30,

Gardiner earned 42 shutouts during his tragedy-shortened career.

Chicago finished second in the American division and Charlie was third in the league in GA average (2.52). By 1931–32, Chicago was still struggling to build a contender, but Gardiner was at the top of his game, capturing his first Vezina Trophy with a league-leading 1.92 GA average. In 316 NHL games, he had a 112–152–52 record with 42 shutouts and a 2.02 GAA.

Gardiner reached his pinnacle in 1933–34—tragically just as his health began to fail. The 'Hawks finished second in the regular season and eliminated the Maroons and Habs before facing Detroit in the best-of-five finals. In Game One, Gardiner held Detroit to one goal in an epic 2–1 double OT win. Chicago sailed to a 4–1 win in the next game, but Gardiner, suffering the effects of his illness, gave up five goals in Game Three. He won the last game of his life in Game Four, a championship effort worthy of earning him entry into the Hall of Fame, which he gained in 1945.

Mike Gartner

No player in the history of the NHL—not Wayne Gretzky, Gordie Howe, Rocket Richard, or anybody else—has achieved what Mike Gartner achieved when he built a streak of 15 consecutive 30-goal seasons, starting with his rookie season (1979–80) when he ripped 36 goals, and ending with the 32 goals he scored in

Gartner has quietly joined the NHL elite with his unassuming, consistent play.

1993–94. His unique and remarkable streak ended in 1994–95, during the lockout-shortened season, when he scored just 12 times in 38 games.

On October 14, 1991, as a member of the New York Rangers, he scored the 500th goal of his career—against his former teammates, the Washington Caps. Later in the same season he notched the 1,000th point of his career.

Michael Alfred Gartner (born October 29, 1959) grew up in the Ottawa area and was an outstanding player in junior hockey during two years at Niagara Falls in the OHA. He scored 74 goals and 165 points in 126 games covering two seasons and established his credentials as a goal-scoring threat. Ineligible to enter the NHL, he turned pro at 19 with the WHA Cincinnati Stingers, scoring 27 goals. On the strength of that performance, he became the fourth player picked overall (by Washington) in the 1979 entry draft, effectively jumping straight from juniors to the WHA to the NHL without stopping in the minors—a privilege generally reserved for the elite.

A speedy skater with a rocket-launcher shot, Gartner immediately proved he could compete, ripping 36 rookie goals. In 1984–85, he had his best season, reaching the 50-goal, 100-point mark for the only time in his career. Traded to the North Stars in 1989, he then moved on to the Rangers in 1990. He scored 49 goals on Broadway in 1990–91, but was traded to Toronto late in the 1993–94 season, just before the Rangers won their first Stanley Cup in 54 years.

Gartner had the misfortune to play the early part of his career in the shadows of Guy Lafleur, Mike Bossy, and Jari Kurri—three of the greatest right wingers ever to skate in the NHL—and yet he joins them, statistically, as one of the most productive snipers in league history. With consistency and durability, Gartner placed himself in that group even though he has never won a single major NHL award.

Following the 1994–95 season he ranked as the fifth all-time leading goal-scorer with 629 career tallies. The only right winger in history to score more goals than Gartner is Gordie Howe, and only Howe, Lafleur, and Kurri have more points among right wingers.

Bernie Geoffrion

One of the early proponents of the slap shot, Bernie Geoffrion was a muscular winger who skated with the Canadiens and Rangers during the 1950s and 1960s. He earned his nickname ("Boom Boom") from the sound that came from his stick hitting the puck (Boom) and the puck crashing into the boards (Boom).

Geoffrion had enormous talent but existed amid controversy throughout his career. In 1954–55 he won his first of two scoring titles, but was unmercifully booed in his own arena, the Montreal Forum, by fans who felt he had unfairly usurped Maurice "Rocket" Richard. Richard was on pace to win his only Art Ross Trophy when NHL boss Clarence Campbell banned him for punching a referee. During the Rocket's absence, Geof-

"The Boomer" won the Calder, the Hart, and two Art Ross Trophies.

frion captured the scoring title—and became the most hated man in Montreal.

Bernard Geoffrion (born February 14, 1931) was always an overachiever. He played Junior A hockey in Montreal when he was just 14, competing against players much older and more developed than himself—but not better. The Habs, in whose minor-league system Geoffrion apprenticed, brought him—and the slapshot—to the NHL at age 19. In 1951–52, he scored 30 goals and won the Calder Trophy as rookie of the year. Just three years later, he led the league in goals (38) and points (75) to capture his first scoring title.

Between 1953 and 1960, he helped the Habs win six Stanley Cups, including five straight (1956–60). He set up the Rocket's Cup-winner in 1956 and Dickie Moore's Cup-winner in 1957. He scored the Cup-clinching goal himself in 1958, added a pair of goals in the finale of the 1959 playoffs against Toronto, and set up Jean Beliveau's Cup-winning

goal in Game Four of the 1960 finals against the Leafs.

On March 3, 1961, he scored against Toronto goalie Cesare Maniago to become only the second player in NHL history to notch 50 goals in a season—joining Habs legend Richard, who did it in 1944–45. However, instead of receiving accolades as a conquering hero, Boom Boom was again derided in Montreal. Fans demeaned his feat, saying Rocket had done it in 50 games while Geoffrion needed 70 games. Nevertheless he won his second Art Ross Trophy and was named MVP.

Citing health problems, Geoffrion retired in 1964 to take up coaching. But the lure of playing was too great, and he made a successful comeback with the Rangers in 1966–67, scoring 17 goals. He quit for good in 1968 with 393 goals and 822 points in 883 NHL games spanning 16 seasons. A six-time Cup winner, Geoffrion (whose son, Danny, played briefly in the NHL) joined the Hall of Fame in 1972.

Michel Goulet

On February 16, 1992, skating for the Chicago Blackhawks, Michel Goulet fired a shot against Calgary's goalie Jeff Reese that bent the twine and lit the red lamp. As the hometown crowd rejoiced, the puck was retrieved and stashed safely away. Goulet, an elegant skater with a muscular finesse, had just scored the 500th goal of his NHL career, joining only 16 other skaters in the game's history to realize such an achievement.

A three-time First Team All-Star, Goulet ruled the NHL during the early to mid-1980s, when he set records for goals by a left winger and was widely viewed as the cream of the crop at his position.

Michel Goulet (born April 21, 1960) was a junior hockey sensation during his second year skating for his hometown Quebec Remparts in 1977–78. Just 17 years old, he scored 73 goals in 72 games, finishing with 135 points. Too young for the NHL draft, he turned pro with the Birmingham Bulls of the WHA, a rugged penalty-filled lineup known more for brawling than scoring. As one of the "Baby Bulls," Goulet scored 28 goals. In 1979, he was drafted by the Quebec Nordiques, who had just become members of the NHL, and he began his 15-year career.

In 1982–83, his fourth season in the league, Goulet hit the 50-goal mark for the first time, ripping 57 goals and beginning a streak during which he enjoyed four consecutive 50-goal seasons; from between 1982–86, he scored 57, 56, 55, and 53 goals.

Goulet banged his way to four consecutive 50-goal seasons (1982-86).

The Nordiques grew steadily into a contender, finishing atop the Adams Division in 1985–86. That year Goulet, with his third 100-point season in four years, earned his second berth on the First All-Star Team. Toward the end of the 1980s, the Nords began to fade, finishing last in the league standings three years in a row. Attempting to unload big salaries, management discarded Goulet, trading him to Chicago during the 1989–90 season for three players who never made an impact on the NHL level.

In Chicago, Goulet put together three 20-goal seasons before disaster struck. On March 16, 1994, at Montreal, he crashed head first into the boards and suffered what turned into a career-ending concussion. Goulet retired prior to the 1994–95 season with 548 goals and 1,152 points in 1,089 games. Though he never won a major NHL award, Goulet currently stands third all-time in goals and points by a left winger.

Wayne Gretzky

The English language hardly contains enough hyperbole to accurately or completely portray the exploits and achievements of Wayne Gretzky, simply the greatest player ever to lace on skates and compete in the NHL. The Great One's imprint on the game has been apparent on the ice, at the box office, and in the record books, with equal effect in every category.

The only award Gretzky never captured (aside from those designated for goalies and defensemen) was the rookie-of-the-year award— and that technicality was derived from his experience in the WHA prior to making his NHL debut in 1979. He owns more than 60 scoring records for regular season, playoff, career, and single-game accomplishments.

He is the game's all-time leading goal-scorer with 814 goals and 2,506 points in 1,173 games—more than two points per game over a career! Furthermore, not only did he

revive hockey in California (a herculean task by itself), he also took the Los Angeles Kings to the brink of a most unlikely Stanley Cup championship when they battled the Canadiens in 1993, losing three games in sudden-death overtime before surrendering in five games.

Wayne Gretzky (born January 26, 1961) was a child prodigy on the rinks of Ontario. Right from the beginning he played against and scored regularly on much older and more experienced competition. Patterning himself after his hero, Gordie Howe, young Gretzky wore the

The Great One has won the coveted NHL scoring crown 10 times.

number 9 jersey of his idol, then switched to the more unique double–9 that would become his trademark.

He played just one year of major junior hockey in Canada, with the Sault Ste. Marie Grey-

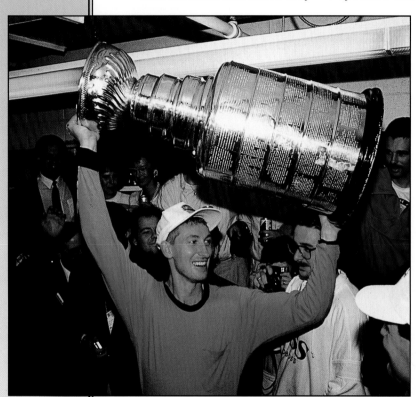

Gretzky led the way to four Stanley Cup championships with Edmonton.

hounds of the Ontario junior league. At age 16, he scored 70 goals and chalked up 182 points in 64 games—nearly three points per game!

With a huge future guaranteed in professional hockey, he left the junior ranks to sign a lucrative million dollar con-

tract with Indianapolis of the WHA. Gretzky was just 17 at the time, and it was a time of much chaos in the rival league. Barely into his first pro season, he was sold to Edmonton tycoon Peter Pocklington. He had played just eight games with Indy before transferring to the Oilers, where he finished the year by scoring 43 goals and 104 points in 72 games. He was voted the WHA rookie of the year on the strength of those impressive statistics. But the best was still awaiting him.

When the Oilers joined the NHL the following year, Gretzky proved he was no fluke. He notched 137 points, tying veteran Marcel Dionne for the league lead, but losing the scoring title—and the chance to win his first Art Ross Trophy—to Dionne (who outscored him 53 to 51). The rookie-of-the-year award—for which Gretzky did not qual-

ify—was given that year to a husky young defenseman from the Quebec major junior ranks: Raymond Bourque.

If he was disappointed by his failure to win the scoring title as a rookie, Gretzky didn't show it. He simply went out and won the next seven scoring championships, setting new and unbelievable scoring records along the way. In 1982, he passed the 200-point mark, making him the first NHLer ever to do so. That year he also set a single-season record for goals (92), which has only been approached—but never matched—by a select group of players (Mario Lemieux scored 85 goals in 1988–89; Brett Hull scored 86 goals in 1990–91).

On August 9, 1988, after nine brilliant seasons in Edmonton—during which he had helped the Oilers win four Stanley Cups—Gretzky was dealt from one of the most powerful teams in the NHL to one of the weakest. The L.A. Kings signed Gretzky in a deal that saw eight players change organizations and $15 million in cash leave the accounts of Kings owner Bruce McNall to fill the Oilers depleted coffers.

Not only did Gretzky face the challenge of helping a new team that lacked the supporting cast the Oilers had always enjoyed, he also had to find a way to save hockey in southern California, which was on the brink of extinction. Of course, number 99 did just that. Not only did he revive interest in the game, he turned California into a hockey hotbed ready to support expansion teams in San Jose and Anaheim.

The only skater ever to reach the 200-point plateau, Gretzky's done it four times (with 212 points in 1981–82, 205 points 1983–84, 208 points in 1984–85, and 215 points in 1985–86). After his streak of seven straight scoring titles, he was knocked off the leader board by Lemieux in 1988 and 1989, but Gretzky was right back in the hunt with his eighth Art Ross title in 1990, and a ninth in 1991. After another two-year layoff, he captured his 10th scoring title in 1993–94 when he led the league with 130 points.

Among his other achievements are nine Hart Trophies as the game's most valuable player; a pair of Conn Smythe Trophies as most valuable playoff performer; five Lester Pearson Awards (voted by the players for MVP); and four Lady Byng Trophies for sportsmanship.

In 1992–93, during his fifth season with the Kings, Gretzky—who'd missed much of the regular season with a very worrisome and potentially

career-threatening back injury—nearly pulled off the impossible. With the Kings barely finishing the regular season at .500 (with a 39–35–10 record), they entered the playoffs as a third-place team, facing the heavily favored Calgary Flames. The Kings found hidden resources and outscored the Flames, 33–28, in a wild shootout series that lasted six games before L.A. took the series with a 9–6 home-ice win. The Kings then took on Vancouver, needing another six games to capture the Division title and earn the right to play Toronto for the conference championship. The Maple Leafs played it tough, and Gretzky was in a do-or-die battle with feisty Doug Gilmour throughout the series, but in a dramatic seventh game, it was Gretzky's hat trick that put the Kings over the top and into the finals.

The Montreal Canadiens, who were in the middle of an incredible overtime winning streak (they'd win 10 straight in sudden death before the

playoffs ended), proved too tough for the Kings. But Gretzky had taken the team to a height never before experienced, and though they failed to capture that elusive championship, the legend of number 99 only grew more stately as a result of the struggle.

George Hainsworth

Short, pudgy, and hardly resembling an athlete at all, goalie George Hainsworth had one of the hardest acts to follow in the history of the NHL. In the aftermath of the sudden death of goaltending legend Georges Vezina, whose greatness in nets inspired a trophy in his name, the Montreal Canadiens found themselves in dire trouble after the 1925–26 season, having gambled on Herb Rheaume and Al Lacroix—and lost. Hainsworth, a Toronto native, stepped into the Habs' nets in 1926–27, a rookie at the age of 31, and was nothing short of sensational, leading the league in goals-against average (1.52) and shutouts (14) and winning the first-ever Vezina Trophy as the NHL's outstanding puckstopper.

George Hainsworth (born June 26, 1895) bounced around the minor leagues for many years before getting a chance to play in the NHL. He didn't begin his career with Montreal until he was 31—an age when most players were past their prime and considering retirement.

Despite his unathletic build—he stood just 5'6" and weighed in at 150 pounds—Hainsworth was a courageous brick wall in goal, playing consistently year after year. As a sophomore in 1927–28, he led the league in wins (26) and GA average (1.09) and won his second Vezina Trophy. During the 1928–29 season, he recorded the second-longest shutout sequence in history when he played more than 343 minutes of hockey without giving up a single goal. That year, he finished the campaign with 22 shutouts and a microscopic 0.98 GA average—both of which stand as the finest marks in the history of the league—and earned his third consecutive Vezina Trophy.

He captured a pair of Stanley Cup titles, in 1930 and 1931, and won 166 of 314 regular season games in seven seasons before he was traded to his hometown Maple Leafs in 1933–34. He played three solid years for the Leafs, twice leading the NHL in wins (26 in 1933–34, and 30 in 1934–35). He took Toronto to the Stanley Cup finals in 1934–35, but his mates couldn't overcome Alex Connell at the other end of the rink, and they lost in three straight. Hainsworth took the Leafs back to the finals the next year, 1935–36, but Norm

Brilliant in goal, Hainsworth won consecutive Vezina Trophies in his first three seasons.

Smith was the better puckstopper that year. Hainsworth gave up an uncharacteristic nine goals in Game Two, and the Leafs went down in four.

Hainsworth returned to Montreal in 1936–37 before retiring. His career GA average (1.91) is the best ever, and he's second all-time in shutouts (94). Hainsworth entered the Hall of Fame in 1961.

Glenn Hall

Unlike his predecessor, Georges Vezina (the first "great" goalie of the NHL, who was known as the "Chicoutimi Cucumber" for his cool demeanor), Glenn Hall, an iron man of unparalleled achievement, became known as "Mr. Goalie" for his superior puckstopping. Off the ice, however, he was also famous for a nervous condition that resulted in his getting physically ill before every game. In fact, it was believed that the sicker Hall got before the game, the better he played once the puck was dropped.

Glenn Henry Hall (born October 3, 1931) hailed from Saskatchewan, son of a western Canadian railway engineer. Discovered by the Red Wings

The very definition of reliability, Hall played in every game for seven straight seasons.

in 1949, Hall moved to Ontario to play for the Windsor Bulldogs, Detroit's junior team. In 1950–51, he was the OHL's most valuable player. From 1951 to 1955, Hall apprenticed in the minors, unable to usurp Terry Sawchuk in the Red Wings' goal.

He finally got his chance in 1955–56, when Sawchuk was traded to Boston. If there were any doubts about Hall's readiness, he erased them with a brilliant rookie season, winning 30 games, leading the league in shutouts (12), and recording an impressive 2.11 GA average, all of which contributed to his winning the Calder Trophy as top rookie.

From 1955 to 1963, Hall played an incredible 502 consecutive games, more than any other goalie in NHL history. In 1957, he was part of a blockbuster trade that sent him to Chicago with Ted Lindsay for Johnny Wilson and others. As a Blackhawk, Hall was no less brilliant. In 1960–61, after a third-place regular season finish, he guided the 'Hawks

through a playoff odyssey that began with a first-round upset of Montreal and ended with a six-game series win over Detroit and a Stanley Cup. Hall's 2.25 playoff GA average was tops, as were his pair of shutouts.

Hall won his first Vezina Trophy in 1962–63 when he led the league in wins (30) and shutouts (five). Later, when Chicago went to a two-goalie system, he won his second Vezina Trophy (in 1966–67), then added a third in 1968–69 as a member of the St. Louis Blues, with whom he finished his 18-year NHL career.

Hall and Jacques Plante gave the expansion Blues a powerful goaltending tandem in 1967–68, taking St. Louis to the Stanley Cup finals. The Blues lost to Montreal in four straight games, but Hall's performance earned him the Conn Smythe Trophy as playoff MVP. Hall is second all-time in games by a goalie (906), third in shutouts (84), and fourth in wins (407). He entered the Hall of Fame in 1975.

Doug Harvey

A funny thing happened in 1958–59: Montreal's Doug Harvey did not win the Norris Trophy as the game's outstanding defenseman. Instead it was his teammate, Tom Johnson, who captured the honor. What was unusual about this circumstance? It was the only time between 1955 and 1962 that Harvey didn't earn the trophy. To date, his seven selections as top defender are second only to the eight won by Bobby Orr of the Boston Bruins.

A player whose puckhandling skills helped revolutionize the position years before Orr came along, Harvey was a great playmaking backliner, a man who could cover his own end and be a weapon in the offensive zone as well.

Douglas Norman Harvey (born December 19, 1924) was destined from childhood to play in Montreal, his hometown. A top amateur player with the Royals, he signed with the Habs in the late 1940s and joined them for good in 1948–49. He was far from an instant hit in Montreal, where fans loathed his lazy appearance on the ice. Despite his great talent, he was a master of economy-of-motion, rarely chasing the puck. Once he had the rubber on his stick, it was his. A tremendous passer, he would control games with his brilliant timing.

In 1952–53, he won his first Stanley Cup, and in 1954–55, he took his first of seven Norris Trophies (in eight years). In winning his initial Norris, he led all NHL defenders in assists (43) and was second only to teammate Bert Olmstead (48) among all players. Harvey's 49 points led all defensemen that year.

In 1956–57, he again led all NHL defenders in assists (44) and points (50) as he garnered his third Norris. He led defensemen in scoring for the last time in 1960–61 when he finished with 39 points and took his sixth Norris Trophy.

After his initial Stanley Cup title in 1953, Harvey was a member of five more Stanley Cup champions from 1955 to 1960. He went to the New York Rangers in 1961–62, where he served as a player-coach and won his final Norris Trophy—an honor he accepted somewhat grudgingly, openly admitting his skills were on the wane.

Harvey, who was known for his wit and relaxed attitude about life and hockey, retired from active duty in 1964. When the NHL expanded from six teams to 12 in 1967–68, he took a second look and made a successful comeback with St. Louis—at the age of 43—in 1968–69. After a few additional seasons in the minors, Harvey called it quits. He was voted into the Hall of Fame in 1973.

In honor of Harvey's contributions, Montreal retired his number (2) in 1985.

Dale Hawerchuk

There is no greater pressure a young NHL prospect can carry on his shoulders than the burden of being picked first overall in the annual entry draft. In the summer of 1981, Dale "Ducky" Hawerchuk felt that weight as the Winnipeg Jets, a struggling NHL franchise just three years removed from its heyday in the defunct WHA, picked him to open the draft. However, a year later, the monkey was off his back. In 1981–82, Hawerchuk set a franchise record for goals (45) and points (103) by a rookie and was the easy pick for the Calder Trophy as the NHL's top first-year player. His 103 rookie points stand as third all-time in the record books behind Teemu Selanne's 132 rookie points in 1992–93 and Peter Stastny's 109 rookie points in 1980–81.

Dale Hawerchuk (born April 4, 1963) grew up in the Toronto area, but instead of finding his place among junior players in the Ontario league, he played in Quebec for the Cornwall Royals. In his first year (1979–80), he had a very respectable 103 points in 72 games and was the QMJHL rookie of the year. The following year, he erupted with 81 goals and 183 points in the same amount of games. For his achievements he was named the Canadian Major Junior Player of the Year.

As an NHLer, Hawerchuk spent much of his early career as the only beacon of light on a dull Jets team that struggled for victories. While he notched 100-point seasons in six of his first seven seasons, the team finished with a winning record only twice in that span and never once survived the playoffs, losing in the first or second round. A masterful playmaker and a gritty performer, Ducky is tougher than he appears, although he is far from a bashing, crashing centerman. An elegant passer, he has radar instincts for his linemates and a hair trigger when it comes to unleashing the puck.

Over the years, he has enjoyed some outstanding moments, such as March 6, 1984, when his Jets bombarded the Kings 7–3. In the second period of that game, Hawerchuk set up five goals, making him the only player in league history to collect five assists in a single period.

In 1990, he was packaged to Buffalo for Phil Housley. As a Sabre he has kept up his excellent scoring, though at a diminished pace, while battling nagging injuries. When the 1994–95 season ended he was just 11 goals shy of 500 for his career. At the time, he boasted 1,314 points in 1,055 games.

Hawerchuk led Winnipeg in scoring all nine years he played there.

Tim Horton

Though he stood only 5'10" and weighed in at 180 pounds, Tim Horton was, in many ways, a gentle giant during his 24 years of NHL hockey. A man of stunning physical strength, he nonetheless played a clean, hard-nosed game and rarely went out of his way to inflict unnecessary pain and suffering on his brethren around the league. When a car accident claimed his life on February 21, 1974, the hockey world united in sadness, remembering a man whose enthusiasm and intensity on the ice had been surpassed only by his popularity among fans and fellow players.

Myles Gilbert Horton (born January 12, 1930) began his hockey playing career as a child in Cochrane, Ontario, but he got his first big break when his family moved to Sudbury and, at 17, he earned a scholarship to St. Michaels in Toronto (a school known for its Junior A hockey program, which sent many players to the NHL). After two successful years of junior hockey, he signed a pro contract with the Maple Leafs' minor league club in Pittsburgh, where he spent three years and helped the team win the 1952 AHL championship Calder Cup.

In 1952–53, Horton earned a regular job with the Maple Leafs, playing 70 games. His hard-hitting play on the blue-line made him a crowd pleaser, and he seemed headed for greatness until, at the end of the 1954–55 season, he suffered a broken leg and jaw in a huge mid-ice collision with Rangers defensive ace Bill Gadsby. It took Horton all summer and much of the next season to recover. Though it took

Horton is tied with Alex Delvecchio for second all-time in seasons played (24).

him a couple of seasons to recapture his form, he eventually became the Leafs' foremost defenseman, a cornerstone to their championship teams of the early 1960s.

With Horton, the Leafs won three straight Stanley Cups from 1961–62 to 1963–64. He collected the first assist on Dick Duff's Stanley Cup-winning goal against Chicago in 1962. After a five-year drought, Horton enjoyed a fourth and final Cup in 1967, just before the NHL expanded from six to 12 teams.

Acquired by the Rangers in 1970, Horton spent one full season on Broadway before moving to Pittsburgh (1971–72), then on to Buffalo (1972–73). On February 21, 1974, the 44-year-old veteran was killed instantly when he lost control of his car en route from Buffalo to his home in Toronto.

Horton's NHL career featured 115 goals and 518 points along with 1,611 penalty minutes in 1,446 games—and four Stanley Cups. He was voted into the Hall of Fame in 1977.

Gordie Howe

Were it not for the amazing grace and scoring wizardry of Wayne Gretzky (whose career was just getting started as Gordie Howe's was ending), there is no doubt that Howe would still reign as the greatest player who ever lived. Howe played an astonishing 26 seasons of NHL hockey plus six more in the rival World Hockey Association. Playing into his 50s, Howe was still getting the job done in 1979–80 when he made a dramatic return to the NHL, proving that even Father Time could not slow him down. Years earlier, at the age of 35 (and playing in his 17th NHL season), Howe demonstrated that he was on top of his game by capturing the sixth scoring title of his career, leading the league with 38 goals and 86 points.

Howe was one of the NHL's most dominant right wingers—if not the preeminent right winger—even during an era that featured Maurice "The Rocket" Richard skating for the rival Montreal Canadiens. Howe led the NHL in goals five times, including three years straight (1951–53) and twice more in 1956–57 and 1962–63. He was voted to the First All-Star Team a dozen times, and when he didn't make the First Team, he was a Second Team selection nine other times. Powerfully built at six feet and tipping the scales at just over 200 pounds, Howe was rock hard and tough as tanned cowhide. Predominantly a right-handed shooter, he was ambidextrous enough to switch hands and shoot lefty if the defense or the goalie offered him no other option. And unlike many great scorers, Howe was not an all-finesse player, proving time and time again that he was capable of becoming a ferocious fighter when provoked. Often, as Howe

went, so went his Detroit Red Wings. On no less than six occasions (1952, 1953, 1957, 1958, 1960, and 1963) he was awarded the Hart Trophy as the league's most valuable player.

Gordon Howe (born March 31, 1928) was a teenage farm boy playing junior hockey in his native Saskatchewan when the New York Rangers first

"Mr. Hockey" played in an astonishing 1,767 NHL games.

spotted him and considered him for the NHL. The Rangers scouts decided young Gordie's skating skills were not up to professional standards, so they sent him back to Saskatoon. Soon thereafter, a Red Wings scout visiting the area watched Howe play, recognized the raw talent, and immediately reported back to the Red Wings, who brought Howe to Ontario. The future legend played briefly on Detroit's junior team in the Ontario junior league before turning pro at just 17. During the 1945–46 season, the emerging star skated for the Red Wings' farm team in Omaha, where he scored 22 goals and notched 48 points. That debut pro season was all the Red Wings needed to be convinced. For Howe, it was his first and only year of minor pro hockey.

The Red Wings promoted Howe to the big leagues in 1946–47, and he never looked back. Although he scored just seven rookie goals, he was a quick learner, playing for coach Jack Adams on a team that featured playmaking

geniuses Billy Taylor and Sid Abel and goal-scoring leader Roy Conacher. As a sophomore in 1947–48, he was teamed with Abel and Ted Lindsay on a line that would one day earn legendary status. But still

Howe was the all-time king in goals, points, and assists—until Wayne Gretzky usurped his throne.

Howe's play was only modest by all measures. In fact, Howe didn't "emerge" until the 1949–50 season when he scored 35 goals (second only to Montreal rival Richard, who had 43) and 68 points, trailing only his linemates Lindsay (78 points) and Abel (69) in the

overall league scoring race.

During the 1950 playoffs, Howe's up-and-coming career—as well as his life itself—nearly came to a tragic end in the team's first-round opener against Toronto when the burly right winger tripped and crashed head first into the dasher boards, suffering a fractured skull. After life-saving surgery to reduce pressure on his wounded brain, Howe began his gradual and total recovery. Though he was unable to rejoin his teammates in those post-season battles, Howe got his name on the Stanley Cup for the first time on April 23, 1950, when Detroit won the championship in a dramatic double-overtime victory over the New York Rangers—the same team that passed on Howe just five years earlier.

Though his injury was serious, it didn't take long for Howe to regain his form. In 1950–51, he captured his first Art Ross Trophy as NHL scoring champ, winning the hockey trifecta with top numbers in goals (43), assists (43), and points (86). Howe's forward

A perfect combination of speed, skill, and strength earned Howe 21 post-season All-Star honors (12 of which were First Team selections).

trio, with Abel and Lindsay, had become known as the "Production Line" and was one of the most feared in the game. With these linemates, Howe established his dominance, leading the Red Wings to three more Stanley Cup championships, beating the powerful Montreal Canadiens in 1952, 1954, and 1955. During the Red Wings' final championship playoff season (1955), Howe led all playoff scorers with nine goals and 20 points in 11 games. To finish his heroics in the grandest style, No. 9 scored the Cup-clinching goal against Montreal's ace goalie, Jacques Plante, with just 11 seconds to play in the second period of Game Seven, giving Detroit a 2–0 lead. (Detroit's Alex Delvecchio and Montreal's Floyd Curry traded third-period goals as the Red Wings held on for a 3–1 win.)

Howe retired in 1971 as the NHL's all-time leading scorer (786 goals, 1,809 points), then made a startling comeback in the WHA, playing on a line with his sons Mark and Marty. In 1979–80, he returned to the NHL—at the age of 51—playing 80 games for Hartford. He finished with 801 goals and 1,850 points in 1,767 games, records that held up until Wayne Gretzky came along. Still considered by some historians as the greatest all-around performer the NHL has ever known, Howe was voted into the Hall of Fame in 1972.

Bobby Hull

Bobby Hull, known as the "Golden Jet" for his blond locks and blinding speed on the rink, was not the first proponent of the slapshot in the 1960s, he was simply its most awesome practitioner.

On March 3, 1962, he blasted a puck past New York Rangers goalie Gump Worsley in the final game of the 1961–62 season, and at just 23 became the youngest man (and the third in NHL history) to reach the 50-goal plateau. Before him, only Rocket Richard (1944–45) and Bernie Geoffrion (1960–61) had reached that magic number. Hull added four more 50-goal seasons before he was through, and helped the Blackhawks win a Stanley Cup in 1960–61.

Robert Marvin Hull (born January 3, 1939) began skating at the age of four on the Bay of Quinte (near Kingston, Ontario), and started organized hockey at 10. At 14 he left home to play Junior B hockey, winning his first league title and tasting the thrill of victory. At 16 he began his Junior A career with the St. Catherines Teepees, a Blackhawks property. His independent nature led to squabbles with his coach, but he produced on the score sheet, and by 1957—at just 18—he was deemed ready for the NHL. His rookie season was unspectacular, with just 13 goals in 70 games, but by his third year (1959–60) he had "arrived," leading the NHL in goals (39) for the first of seven times.

Hull won the Art Ross Trophy as scoring champ three times (1960, 1962, and 1966) and was a two-time Hart Trophy winner as league MVP (1965 and 1966). His 14 points in 12 playoff games in 1961 helped seal the playoff championship, as did his assist on Ab McDonald's Cup-clinching goal against Detroit in Game Six.

During the 1960s, Hull was the 'Hawks most productive scorer, their fastest skater, their hardest shooter, and their busiest player (typically playing up to 40 minutes per game). But in 1972 he left Chicago to chase the big money of the WHA (becoming the first million dollar hockey player). Latching on with Winnipeg, he continued his awesome scoring, reaching a career-high 77 goals in 1974–75. The highest goal-scoring left winger in NHL history, Hull played seven seasons in the WHA, winning three league playoff titles, before returning for a swan song in the NHL in 1979–80. He retired with 610 NHL goals and 1,170 points. He added 303 goals and 638 points during his tenure in the WHA. His son, Brett, considered one of the NHL's foremost snipers, skates for the St. Louis Blues and has already made the Hulls hockey's only father-son 50-goal threat. Bobby Hull entered the Hall of Fame in 1983.

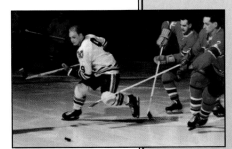

Hull was the first player to score more than 50 goals in one season (54 in 1965-66).

Brett Hull

The record crept slowly upward: Flyer right winger Reggie Leach had 61 goals in 1975–76. Then Islander Mike Bossy ripped 69 in 1978–79. Edmonton's Jari Kurri upped the ante to 71 goals in 1984–85. Finally, St. Louis right winger Brett Hull moved ahead with 72 goals in 1989–90. But after years of watching the record shift in tiny increments, suddenly Hull— "Golden Brett," son of the great Golden Jet, Bobby Hull— shattered his own mark when he blasted 86 goals in 1990–91, the most ever in a single season by a right winger, and the third most goals by any player in a season (after Wayne Gretzky's 92 and 87).

During a span of time from 1989 to 1994, no NHLer scored more goals than Hull (339). In his first 540 games he ripped 413 goals and 700 points, a pace that should land him in the Hall of Fame when his brilliant playing career concludes.

Brett Hull (born August 9, 1964) was raised in Belleville, Ontario (where his father had a cattle farm during his off-seasons). Brett's rise to dominance as an NHLer was not always a foregone conclusion—even in light of his heritage. As a teenager, he was a lazy player with poor work habits. In 1982, at 18, when most players were setting their sights on the NHL, Hull was on his way to Junior B hockey in British Columbia. At Penticton, he blossomed, scoring 153 goals and 292 points in 106 games

Golden Brett Hull holds the Blues team record for career goals.

during two seasons, which earned him a spot with the Bulldogs of the University of Minnesota-Duluth. At the same time, he was drafted by Calgary, 117th overall, in the 1984 draft. After two years at UMD,

where he was a WCHA all-star, he joined the Flames. But even after winning AHL rookie-of-the-year honors with a 50-goal season at Moncton, he struggled for ice time with Calgary.

Toward the end of the 1987–88 season, he was traded to St. Louis, where he finished his first 30-goal season. In 1988–89, he ripped 41 goals and 84 points and it was off to the races. The following season he led the league in goals (72) and won the Lady Byng Trophy (24 PIM). In 1990–91, he again topped all NHL goal-scorers (86) and captured MVP honors both from writers, with the Hart Trophy, and among his own peers, with the Lester B. Pearson Award. He led the league in goals a third time in 1991–92 (70).

A three-time NHL First All-Star Team right winger, Hull reigns as the NHL's top gun, mixing accuracy, velocity, and the quickest trigger around. His game is very different from his father's, but like his dad, Brett is destined for the Hall of Fame.

Aurel Joliat

In perhaps the greatest compliment one player could ever pay another, the superb Howie Morenz of the Montreal Canadiens once told the world that were it not for his centerman, Aurel Joliat, a spry hint of a physical specimen who dazzled with speed and grace, Morenz's own career would never have taken on such great proportions.

Joliat, a 16-year veteran with the Canadiens, was tiny by professional sports standards, standing just 5'6" and weighing between 135 and 140 pounds. But beneath his Habs jersey beat the heart of a lion; a competitor whose skills were matched only by his ability to execute and fulfill his tremendous potential.

Aurel Joliat (born August 29, 1901) learned to skate in Ottawa, on the Rideau Canal, where his childhood buddies included the Boucher brothers, Frank and Billy. A talented athlete, Joliat's first pro sports job was as a football star in Saskatchewan, where he suffered an injury that suspended his gridiron career. In 1922, fully healthy, he was acquired by the Canadiens (at the insistence of Billy Boucher) and thus began his Hall of Fame NHL career.

Teamed on a line with Morenz and Boucher, Joliat quickly developed into one of the game's most efficient and productive centermen. In his third season, 1924–25, he finished third in overall scoring with a career-high 40 points. Easily recognizable for the black cap he always wore on the ice, Joliat was a masterful playmaker, finding his linemates with goal-making passes.

Joliat earned his first Stanley Cup title in 1923–24, as a sophomore, as his line destroyed first Vancouver (PCHL) and then Calgary

The Habs traded legend Newsy Lalonde to take a chance on the young, unproven Joliat.

(WCHL) in just four games. He put his name to a second Cup championship in 1929–30, as the Habs ousted Boston in two straight games in the finals.

When Johnny "Black Cat" Gagnon joined the Habs in 1930–31, the newly formed trio of Gagnon-Joliat-Morenz helped the Canadiens forge a successful defense of their league title. Gagnon tied for the playoff goal-scoring lead (six), and Joliat assisted his Cup-clinching goal against Chicago in Game Five of the finals.

In 1933–34, Joliat posted 22 goals and 37 points to earn his only the Art Ross Trophy. He retired in 1938 with 270 goals and 460 points in 654 games and three Stanley Cups. He was elected to the Hall of Fame in 1945.

Red Kelly

Imagine Willie Mays shifting effortlessly from centerfield to shortstop and playing with equal grace and effectiveness. Picture legendary quarterback Johnny Unitas, failing to lead his offense to a first down, staying on the gridiron to lead the defense as a star linebacker. Conjure up these fantastic rotations and you'll understand the greatness of Red Kelly, who won a Norris Trophy as the NHL's top defenseman in 1954, plus four Lady Byng Trophies (1951, 1953, 1954, and 1961), and was also a renowned center later in his career after leaving Detroit for Toronto.

Leonard Patrick Kelly (born July 9, 1927) hailed from Ontario and was one of the

Kelly won four Stanley Cups with Detroit— and four more with Toronto.

legion of famous enrollees at Toronto's St. Michael's College, where he first played alongside future Detroit mate Ted Lindsay. The Maple Leafs had the best chance to scout Kelly, but thought the offense-minded defenseman lacked the skills to make it. Detroit disagreed. In 1947, after three years in the minors, Kelly made his NHL debut, apprenticing under Hall of Famer Bill Quakenbush.

In 1949–50, Kelly led all NHL defensemen in points (40) for the first time, a trick he would turn five more times in the next six years. In 1953–54, he was honored as the first-ever recipient of the James Norris Memorial Trophy.

With Kelly cruising the blue line, the Red Wings captured Stanley Cups in 1950, 1952, 1954, and 1955. By the middle of the 1959–60 season, however, he had run afoul of team boss Jack Adams, who was offering Kelly a contract the red-haired ace thought was unacceptable. Adams tried to trade Kelly to the Rangers for Bill Gadsby, but Kelly refused

to report, threatening instead to retire. Given a five-day period in which to consider his future (retire permanently or resume his career and accept the trade), he gave heavy weight to hanging up his skates, but Toronto called and convinced Kelly to play with the Leafs, where his experience and savvy would be invaluable to the young Toronto club. Kelly made a deal with Adams, who swapped him to the Leafs for Marc Reaume. Coach Punch Imlach immediately installed Kelly—at center!—on a line with Frank Mahovlich and Bob Nevin.

Kelly won four more Stanley Cups, all in Toronto (1962–64 and 1967), before retiring at age 40 with 281 goals and 823 points in 1,316 games. He notched 119 goals and 351 points alone as a center after going to Toronto at the age of 30. One of the most versatile and gentlemanly players in the history of the game, Kelly entered the Hall of Fame in 1969.

Ted Kennedy

Though he accomplished more than most NHLers—including taking the Maple Leafs to a Stanley Cup before his 20th birthday—Ted Kennedy may be best remembered as the man who nearly killed Gordie Howe, without ever laying a glove on him.

On March 28, 1950, at Olympia Stadium, the Red Wings were hosting Toronto in the first game of the Stanley Cup semifinals. In the third period, with the Leafs up 4–0, Howe took a run at Kennedy, missed, and crashed head-first into the boards, suffering a fractured skull that required life-saving surgery. Kennedy was vilified by fans and press, accused of knocking Howe into the boards. Impartial witnesses ultimately cleared Kennedy, who was known as a clean, classy player.

Theodore Kennedy (born December 12, 1925) grew up in Ontario, where he was discovered by former NHL great Nels Stewart while playing junior hockey. Stewart took Kennedy under his wing and later convinced the Maple Leafs to sign the young center. At the age of 17, he signed with Toronto and made his NHL debut late in the 1942–43 season.

In his official rookie year (1943–44), he scored 26 goals and then proved it was no fluke by knocking in 29 more the following year, finishing tied for second in the league. In 1944–45, he led all playoff goal-scorers (seven) as the Leafs marched to the Stanley Cup championship, only their second title since 1932. After failing to qualify for the playoffs in 1945–46, the Leafs were back in 1946–47, the start of an era of dominance that would see them win four of the next five Stanley Cups.

In the 1947 finals, as the Leafs and Habs battled for six games, Kennedy had the game-winner in Game Two and the Cup-clinching goal in Game Six. During the 1948 playoffs, Kennedy led all scorers with eight goals and 14 points as the Leafs swept Detroit in the finals. By 1948–49, the legendary Syl Apps was at retirement age and the Leafs were looking for a new captain. Just 22 years old, "Teeder" Kennedy was designated to wear the captain's "C" on his jersey. The 1949 finals were a replay of the '48 championship round, and the results were the same as Toronto brushed aside the Red Wings in four games; Kennedy led the Leafs with eight points. He took the Leafs to one more title, in 1951, scoring an OT winner in Game Three as the Leafs took the Habs in four games.

Kennedy won the Hart Trophy as MVP in 1955, then retired in 1957 with 231 goals and 560 points in 696 games. He entered the Hall of Fame in 1966.

Teeder played his entire career with the Leafs, leading them to five championships.

Jari Kurri

One could argue that without Wayne Gretzky as his center, Jari Kurri would never have become the prolific scorer he was in his heyday with the Edmonton Oilers. Conversely, however, the argument also could be made that without Kurri's masterful goal-scoring talent, Gretzky would never have amassed the incredible assist numbers he enjoyed during the Oilers' dynasty years of the mid to late-1980s.

Among all-time NHL right wingers, only Gordie Howe and Guy Lafleur have more points than Kurri, and as the 1995–96 season got underway, Kurri needed only 58 points to surpass Lafleur for second place among starboard wingers.

Jari Kurri (born May 18, 1960) was raised in Helsinki, Finland, and found his way to the Finnish senior league at the age of 17. After three seasons with Jokerit, he was drafted by the Oilers in 1980, the same year they drafted Paul Coffey and Andy Moog. Kurri joined the Oilers in

1980–81, was teamed with Gretzky, and blasted 32 rookie goals. He scored 32 goals again as a sophomore, then upped his total to 45 goals in 1982–83. In 1983–84, he reached the 50-goal plateau for the first of four such occasions and won his first Stanley Cup, leading all playoff goal-scorers (14). In 1984–85, he blasted 71 goals—at the time a record for right wingers—and added 19 more in the playoffs as the Oilers won their second Cup.

A devastating shooter who helped popularize the "one-timer"—shooting from the off-wing without stopping the pass, firing directly on net as the feed arrives—Kurri led the

Kurri was the third player in history to score 70 or more goals in one season.

NHL in goals in 1985–86 with 68 tallies. The team's Stanley Cup dynasty was rudely interrupted by Calgary in the playoffs, but the powerful Edmontonians were right back on track in 1986–87 as Kurri notched his fifth straight 100-point season, this time with 54 goals. The Oilers won their third Cup and Kurri again led all playoff goal-scorers (15).

The 1987–88 season was bittersweet for Edmonton. Though they captured their fourth Cup in five years, Kurri's production was down (43 goals), and it would be the final season in Edmonton for Gretzky, who was bound for the Kings. Kurri, winner of the 1985 Lady Byng Trophy, stayed in the Oilers system long enough to win his fifth Cup in 1990, then he played the 1990–91 season in Italy before returning to the NHL. A three-team trade landed him in Los Angeles where he was reunited with Gretzky. With 565 goals and 1,296 points in 1,028 games, Kurri seems destined for the Hall of Fame.

Elmer Lach

Let no comparison of "the old NHL" and the modern-day NHL diminish the great accomplishments of the superstars of yesteryear. When Elmer Lach won his first Art Ross Trophy as the NHL's top scorer in 1944–45, his 80 points in 50 games were the equivalent of a 135-point season in today's game. The 54 assists he accumulated that year set a new standard in the NHL, breaking the previous record held by Chicago's Clint Smith (49). Lach earned his only Hart Trophy as the league's most valuable player that same season and was instrumental in helping his right winger, the great Maurice "Rocket" Richard, enter the record books with the game's first-ever 50-goal season—in only 50 games!

Lach teamed with Richard and left wing sensation Toe Blake to comprise one of the league's deadliest combinations, known as the "Punch Line." In 1947–48, Lach scored a career-high 30 goals and finished second to Detroit's Ted Lindsay (33), but won the scoring title with 61 points.

Elmer James Lach (born January 22, 1918) hailed from the farmland of Saskatchewan where he played organized hockey until the Habs discovered him in the late 1930s. He made his NHL debut in Montreal in 1940–41 with only modest success, then missed the entire 1941–42 season with a broken arm suffered in the season opener. In 1943–44, Rocket Richard replaced Joe Benoit on Lach's right wing, and the newly born "Punch Line" carried the Habs to a league title and their first Stanley Cup in 13 years.

An aggressive, hard-nosed player, Lach also was the recipient of many painful injuries that reduced his effectiveness and kept him from reaching even higher ground in the game's illustrious history.

In 1945–46, he displayed his full potential when he spearheaded the Canadiens to a five-game Stanley Cup finals win over Boston. He led all playoff scorers with 12 assists and 17 points, and assisted on Blake's Cup-clinching goal midway through the third period of Game Five.

Lach's last great moment came seven years later, during the 1953 Stanley Cup finals when he scored his only goal of the post-season, at 1:22 of sudden-death OT in Game Five against Boston, giving the Habs the Cup. Lach retired in 1954 with 215 goals and 623 points in 664 games, a pair of scoring titles, an MVP trophy, and three Stanley Cups. He entered the Hall of Fame in 1966.

Guy Lafleur

On December 20, 1983, the powerful Montreal Canadiens humiliated the lowly New Jersey Devils on their own ice, thrashing them 6–0. The victory itself was not unusual, nor even the manner in which it was achieved. But among the Habs' wrecking crew, Guy Lafleur stood out

"The Flower" bloomed in Montreal, racking up six consecutive 50-goal seasons.

when his goal against Chico Resch became the 500th of his career, making him the 10th NHLer in history—and the fourth Canadien—to reach that hallowed plateau.

Lafleur, a three-time NHL scoring champion, was the key to the Habs' dynamic offense from the mid-1970s until his reign in Montreal came to an

unhappy conclusion early in the 1984–85 season. He won the Conn Smythe Trophy as playoff MVP in 1977 and was a member of five Stanley Cup champions during his 14-year career with Les Habitants.

Guy Damien Lafleur (born September 20, 1951) grew up in Thurso, Quebec, and didn't leave home until he was 15, when he joined the Quebec City Remparts in the Quebec Major Junior League. In 1969–70, his second full season, he scored 103 goals in 56 games and led the team to the first of two straight league and playoff titles. The next year, he won the QMJHL scoring title with 130 goals and 209 points in 62 games and was the first player chosen in the 1971 amateur draft (by Montreal).

He got off to a slow start as an NHLer, playing under the awesome weight of his pre-NHL hype. It wasn't until his fourth season, 1974–75, that he emerged, scoring 53 goals (his first of six straight 50-goal seasons) and 119 points. He won his first of three straight

scoring titles in 1975–76, with 56 goals and 125 points. That year, the Habs won the Stanley Cup, a title they would hold for four consecutive years.

In 1976–77, Lafleur had his best season, with a career-high 135 points. He won the Hart Trophy as MVP as well as the Lester B. Pearson Award (the players' choice for outstanding performer). That year he earned the playoff MVP award as well. As an encore, Lafleur scored 60 goals to lead the NHL in 1977–78 (his career best), and won his third Art Ross Trophy and second Hart Trophy. In 1978–79, he led the Habs to their fourth straight Stanley Cup. A messy retirement born out of a dispute with the Habs kept him on the shelf for three years (1985–88). He was voted into the Hall of Fame in 1988, but he made a triumphant return with the Rangers in 1988–89, then played two more years with Quebec before retiring for good in 1991 with 560 goals and 1,353 points in 1,126 NHL games.

Newsy Lalonde

Long before the NHL was organized as the major hockey league of Canada and the United States, Newsy Lalonde, a fiery French Canadian goal-scoring wizard who dominated his sport during the early years of the 20th century, had already established himself as the preeminent player in all of organized hockey.

A star in the National Hockey Association (the predecessor to the NHL), Lalonde became a scoring champion for the Montreal Canadiens in 1910–11 when he scored an unheard of 38 goals in just 11 games. A gun-for-hire in an era when players were not firm property of the teams for which they played, Lalonde bounced from the NHA to the newly formed Pacific Coast Hockey Association in 1911–12, journeying to Vancouver to compete. He won the first PCHA scoring title with 27 goals. Lalonde then returned to Montreal in 1912 and finished his career on the east coast of Canada. In 1915–16,

he captured yet another scoring title, with 31 goals for the Canadiens in the NHA.

Eduoard Lalonde (born October 31, 1887) hailed from Cornwall, Ontario. He came into the world ominously on Halloween Night, and although he didn't get his first pair of ice skates until he was 15, he later haunted several leagues (including the NHA, PCHL, and NHL) with his scary combination of scoring ability and fierce, sometimes dirty play. Known as much for his puckhandling as for his hot temper, Lalonde was the game's original Charley Hustle.

When the NHL was officially formed in 1917–18, Lalonde initially took a back seat to scoring ace Joe Malone, who scored 44 goals in 20

games (while Newsy had "only" 23 goals in 14 games). Lalonde won his first NHL scoring title in 1918–19 with 32 points in 17 games. Lalonde won another scoring title in 1920–21 when he netted 33 goals and 41 points. He fell off dramatically the following year, with only nine goals, and in 1922 he left the NHL— traded to Saskatoon of the WCHL for a young star named Aurel Joliat.

Lalonde returned to the NHL as a coach in 1926–27, first with the New York Americans, and later with Ottawa (1929–31) and the Canadiens (1932–35), though his successes were few and far between. Lalonde, who scored 441 goals in 365 pro games, including 124 goals in 99 NHL games, entered the Hall of Fame in 1950.

Mario Lemieux

No player in the history of the NHL has earned a higher goals-per-game average than Mario Lemieux. Through 1994–95, Lemieux had scored .825 goals-per-game, nearly a goal a game. Only Wayne Gretzky, with an average of 2.14 points-per-game, has a higher PPG average than Lemieux, who had notched 1,211 points in 599 NHL games for a 2.02 average. Sadly, few superstars in the history of the NHL have endured the physical hardship that plagued Lemieux since he debuted in 1984.

In 1990–91, Lemieux missed all but 26 of the Pittsburgh Penguins' regular season games as back ailments crippled him; yet he notched 45 points and carried the team to its first-ever Stanley Cup. The following season, playing in pain so excruciating that at times he couldn't tie the laces on his own skates, Lemieux played 64 games, won his third scoring title, and took Pittsburgh to their second straight Stanley Cup.

Mario Lemieux (born October 5, 1965) grew up in the outskirts of Montreal and was a child prodigy, playing with much older players and dominating them. In three years at Laval in the Quebec junior league, he scored 247 goals and 562 points in just 200 games—including an astonishing 282 points during his final season, making him Canada's top junior player. As the first pick overall in the 1984 entry draft, Lemieux took the Pittsburgh franchise on his back and began to carry it up the ladder of the NHL standings, starting at the bottom.

As a rookie in 1984–85, Lemieux scored 43 goals and 100 points and won the Calder Trophy. He raised his point total to 141 as a sophomore. In his fourth NHL season (1987–88), he interrupted the seven-year reign of Wayne Gretzky, winning his first of four scoring titles with 70 goals and 168 points. He followed up with 85 goals and 199 points and another Art Ross Trophy in 1988–89.

Lemieux won two more scoring titles (1992 and 1993) and captured three Lester B. Pearson Awards (1986, 1987, and 1992), won a pair of Hart Trophies as the NHL's MVP (1988 and 1993), was twice the MVP in the Stanley Cup playoffs (1991 and 1992), and earned the Masterton Trophy for perseverance in 1993.

A bout with Hodgkins disease in 1992–93 interrupted Lemieux's final Art Ross season, but miraculously he finished with 160 points in 60 games. After missing 62 games in 1993–94 Lemieux quit, vowing not to play again unless his health returned to 100 percent. In 1995–96, Lemieux once again laced up his skates for the Penguins.

Lemieux's career has been a struggle between greatness and adversity.

Ted Lindsay

They didn't call him "Terrible" because he couldn't play the game; instead, it was Ted Lindsay's ferocious approach to the game that earned him his nickname. Whether he was chasing down a loose puck, throwing a big check, or blasting officials with a streak of diatribe, Lindsay lived up to his reputation as one of the game's most fearsome competitors.

For five years (1947–52), Lindsay was the left winger on Detroit's famed "Production Line" with center Sid Abel and right winger Gordie Howe. A multiple threat, Lindsay won a league scoring title, chalked up huge penalty numbers as a scrapper extraordinaire, and helped the Red Wings win four Stanley Cups.

Robert Blake Theodore Lindsay (born July 29, 1925) was the youngest of five sons of former Renfrew (Ontario) Millionaires goalie Bert Lindsay. After moving to Kirkland Lake, Ontario, he played his junior hockey at St. Michael's College in Toronto, and later helped the Oshawa Generals win the 1944 Memorial Cup.

Signed by Detroit, Lindsay made his NHL debut in 1944–45, but didn't establish himself until the assembly of the Production Line in 1947–48. That year, he led the

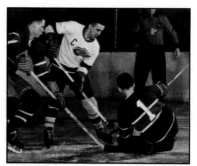

Terrible Ted averaged more than a penalty minute per game (1.69).

league in goals (33) and was top-five in penalty minutes (95). Terrible Ted won his only Art Ross Trophy two years later when he led the NHL in assists (55) and points (78) in 1949–50, despite sitting out 141 penalty minutes (third-highest total in the league). Lindsay finished second to Howe in points in 1951–52 and again the following year.

In the 1952 playoffs, Lindsay led all players in goals (five) and points (seven) as the Red Wings swept Montreal to take their second Cup in three years. In 1955, when Detroit captured its final Stanley Cup title, Lindsay's 12 assists led all playmakers, and he finished with 19 points, one behind Gordie Howe (20) for the playoff lead.

Lindsay ran afoul of Red Wings management in 1957 when he announced the formation of a players' union—the very idea of which horrified owners. Banished to Chicago, the feisty winger spent three years in a Blackhawks sweater, with modest results. He retired in 1960 and spent four years in exile, watching his Detroit-area businesses grow. In 1964–65, he talked the Red Wings into letting him make a comeback. At 39, Lindsay played 69 games with 14 goals and 28 points. He quit for good in 1965 with 379 goals and 851 points (and 1,808 PIM) in 1,068 games. Lindsay went into the Hall of Fame in 1966.

Frank Mahovlich

During his 17-year NHL career, words like "brooding" and "surly" were often used to describe Frank Mahovlich. Other words included "All-Star" and "champion," as in six Stanley Cups—four in Toronto, two in Montreal. Known as "The Big M," the lanky left winger was the fifth player in league history to score 500 goals (and only the second left winger after Bobby Hull to achieve that mark). He was also the eighth NHLer to reach the hallowed 1,000-point plateau.

In 1964, when the Maple Leafs won their third straight Stanley Cup, Mahovlich led the team in scoring with 15 points and led all playoff scorers with 11 assists. Seven years later, in the 1971 playoffs, he notched 14 goals and 27 points to lead all players in both categories, and guided the Canadiens over Chicago in seven games.

Francis William Mahovlich (born January 10, 1938) grew up in Timmins, Ontario, and was the object of every NHL team's desire as a teenager. He eventually chose St. Michael's College, a Catholic high school in Toronto, which ran the Leafs' Junior A team in the OHA. In 1956–57, Mahovlich was the OHA's MVP with 52 goals.

In 1957–58, Mahovlich joined the Leafs on a full-time basis and notched 20 rookie goals, good enough to capture the Calder Trophy. In 1960–61, playing on a line with Red Kelly and Bob Nevin, he emerged as a superstar when he ripped 48 goals, challenging the 50-goal record held to that date only by Montreal's Rocket Richard (who, amazingly, scored that mark in only 50 games!). Mahovlich never

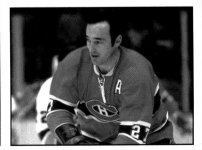

One of the game's greatest left wingers, Mahovlich played on six Cup-winners.

cracked the 50-goal nut, and it became a sore spot with Toronto fans who felt The Big M was not working hard enough to fulfill his obvious potential.

After more than a decade in Toronto—and four Stanley Cup rings—Mahovlich was traded to Detroit in 1968. He spent three seasons with the Wings, scoring 49 goals in 1968–69 while playing on a line with Alex Delvecchio and Gordie Howe. At age 33, he was traded to Montreal late in the 1970–71 season. He soon led the Habs to a pair of Stanley Cups (1971 and 1973), skating with his kid brother, Pete (known as "Little M" despite standing 6'5").

Mahovlich completed his NHL career in 1974, chasing the big bucks of the WHA, where he notched 89 goals and 232 points in 237 games. He hung up his skates in 1978. Ranked fourth all-time among NHL left wingers for goals (533), assists (570), and points (1,103), Mahovlich was voted into the Hall of Fame in 1981.

Joe Malone

The numbers tell the tale: 44 goals in 20 games. In any league, in any era, in any level of competition, those are awesome numbers. And in fact, Joe Malone's NHL-record goals-per-game average (2.2) has never been approached, let alone matched or surpassed. Malone was a hockey superstar before there was an NHL. By the time he debuted with the first-year NHL Canadiens in 1917–18, he was a 27-year-old veteran with a long resume of astonishing scoring wizardry.

Maurice Joseph Malone (born February 28, 1890) was raised in Quebec City, where he began his professional career with the Quebec Bulldogs of the National Hockey

Malone holds the record for single-season goals-per-game (2.20).

Association, the precursor to the NHL. The Bulldogs, a team born out of a merger between two failed clubs, Haileybury and Cobalt, dominated the NHA during the mid-1910s. A quick skater with deft moves, Malone earned the nickname "Phantom" in his NHA days.

In 1911, Malone and the Bulldogs captured the league title and, in an era when the Stanley Cup was a challenge series, defeated Moncton of the Maritime league to win the Cup. In 1912–13, Malone led the league with 43 goals in 20 games as the Bulldogs again won the league title. In the 1912 playoffs, Quebec took on Sydney, Nova Scotia, and Malone ripped nine goals in the first game as the Bulldogs cruised to a 20–5 victory.

Not immune to injuries, Malone had his "off"-seasons as well, such as the 1914–15 season, when he was hobbled for half the year with a bum ankle. In 1916–17, the final year of the NHA's existence, Malone and Ottawa ace Frank Nighbor tied for the league

lead in scoring with 41 goals apiece. In one game that season, Malone scored eight goals against the rival Montreal Wanderers.

In 1917–18, Malone left the Bulldogs to join the Canadiens for the first year of the NHL, which began as a four-team bloc (Ottawa, Toronto, Montreal Wanderers, and—of course—the Habs). On opening night, Malone scored five goals. He finished the year with 44 goals to win the very first Art Ross Trophy as NHL scoring champion. After a dismal 1918–19 season shortened by injury, Malone switched back to the revitalized Quebec Bulldogs in 1919–20 and led the league with 39 goals and 48 points in 24 games, winning his second Ross Trophy. On January 31, 1920, he scored an NHL-record seven goals against Toronto. After two years with Hamilton, he returned to the Habs, where he played from 1922–24, before retiring with 146 goals in 125 NHL games. Malone entered the Hall of Fame in 1950.

Lanny McDonald

What made Lanny McDonald great wasn't his outstanding skating, laser-beam shooting, chippy physical play, or even his colorful Yosemite Sam moustache—all characteristics that defined him during his 16-year NHL career. What made him great was his ability to play a consistently superior brand of hockey regardless of his surroundings. Whether he was playing on a very good team (Toronto, 1973–79), a very bad team (Colorado, 1979–81), or a Stanley Cup-quality team (Calgary, 1981–89), McDonald always contributed a total effort.

As a result, the crusty right winger (who never won a major NHL scoring award) finished his career with 500 goals and 1,006 points, benchmarks of outstanding achievement.

Lanny King McDonald (born February 16, 1953) grew up in rural Alberta, playing his junior hockey in the rugged Western league, helping the Medicine Hat Tigers win the WHL playoff title in 1973 with a league-high 18 goals in 17 playoff games. With 112 goals and 253 points in 136 junior games, McDonald became a coveted prospect and was Toronto's first choice (fourth overall) in the 1973 draft.

He jumped straight to the NHL and spent six-and-a-half years in Toronto, where he skated with Darryl Sittler and Tiger Williams. In 1976–77, he scored 46 goals, then one-upped himself the following year with 47 goals.

Traded to the lowly Colorado Rockies midway through the 1979–80 season, following several playoff disasters in Toronto, McDonald showed he had plenty of hockey left. In 1980–81, his only full season with the Rockies, he banged home 35 goals. Early in the 1981–82 campaign, he was shipped to Calgary, where he finished the season with 40 goals.

In 1982–83, at the age of 30, McDonald had his finest hours. Relying on his rocket-launcher shot and quick release, he blasted a career-

McDonald's 66-goal season with Calgary is a team record.

high 66 goals. With the scoring awards going to Wayne Gretzky, McDonald had to settle for the Masterton Trophy (for perseverance) as recognition of his outstanding display. On March 22, 1984, he scored two goals in six seconds against Detroit, tying three others for the third-fastest pair of goals in NHL history.

In 1989, during the Stanley Cup finals against Montreal, McDonald scored the go-ahead goal in Game Six as Calgary iced its first-ever championship, after which McDonald, 36, announced his retirement. He went into the Hall of Fame in 1992.

Mark Messier

A handful of lucky NHLers have been able to put their names on the Stanley Cup more than once, with different teams, but only one man has ever captained Stanley Cup champions in two cities. That man is Mark Messier, who took the Edmonton Oilers to their fifth playoff title in seven years in 1990 before migrating east to Broadway where he guided the New York Rangers to a Stanley Cup title in 1994, their first championship in 54 years.

After Wayne Gretzky (346), no player in the history of the game has more playoff points than Messier, who finished the 1995 playoff season with 272 points. In 1994–95, the rugged center notched the 100th playoff goal of his career, making him only the third player ever to reach the century mark—along with Gretzky (110) and Jari Kurri (102). He is also the all-time leader in shorthanded playoff goals (14).

Mark Douglas Messier (born January 18, 1961) was born and raised in Edmonton, where his father was a minor league hockey legend. After a very brief junior career (he was 17 when he appeared in seven playoff games for the Portland Winter Hawks in 1978), Mess turned pro with Indianapolis of the WHA in 1978–79, but was shipped to Cincinnati after only five games. He scored one goal in 47 games, but was the Oilers' second pick in the 1979 draft, moving to the NHL with only four games on the farm.

After a 12-goal rookie season, he upped his personal ante to 23 goals in 1980–81, then erupted with 50 goals—his only 50-goal season—in 1981–82. He scored 48 goals the following year and enjoyed his first 100-point season. With the help of the Gretzky-Messier one-two punch, the Oilers finally overcame the Islanders dynasty in 1984, winning their first Stanley Cup. Messier, who notched 26 points in 19 games, was voted the MVP, taking the Conn Smythe Trophy. The Oilers won four Cups from 1984 through 1988, but when Gret-zky left for L.A., doubts swirled in Edmonton. However, Messier led the Oilers to a fifth Cup in 1989–90, and he won the Hart Trophy as the league's MVP and the Lester B. Pearson Award as the players' choice for top performer.

Messier is second all-time in playoff points (272) and assists (170).

Leaving Edmonton for New York in 1991, Messier helped the Rangers win the President's Trophy as the NHL's top regular season finisher in 1991–92, notching 107 points, and once more took both the Hart Trophy and Pearson Award. In 1994, he took command of the Rangers' playoff fortunes, exorcized the demons of 54 years, and delivered the Stanley Cup to Broadway, thus ensuring his place in history.

Stan Mikita

The 1966–67 campaign was a bonanza for Chicago center Stan Mikita, playing in his eighth NHL season. Not only did he win his third league scoring title, with 97 points (setting a new mark for assists, 62, and tying the league record for total points), he also captured the Hart Trophy as the NHL's most valuable player and the Lady Byng Trophy for his sportsmanship. It was the first time in league history that one player had pulled off a triple-crown, winning three major awards in one season. And what made it more remarkable was the fact that only two years earlier, Mikita had been among the league's most penalized players, with 154 PIM.

Stanislav Gvoth (born May 20, 1940) was eight years old, living a poverty-stricken existence in the farming town of Sokolov, Czechoslovakia, when his parents sent him to live with his uncle's family—the Mikita family—in Ontario. Though slight of build, young Stan was an outstanding athlete, excelling in baseball, basketball, football, and hockey. As a teenager, he joined the St. Catherine's Teepees, a junior hockey team operated by the Chicago Blackhawks. He led the OHA in scoring in 1958–59 and finished the year with the NHL team.

As an NHL rookie in 1959–60, the hard-nosed center scored modestly and fought tirelessly. In fact, in his first six NHL seasons, he accumulated 688 penalty minutes and 408 points, proving he could play tough and still get numbers on the board. In the 1960–61 playoffs, the powerful Blackhawks beat Montreal and Detroit to win the Stanley Cup,

In 1961, Mikita brawled his way to Chicago's first Cup win since 1938.

and Mikita's six goals led the 'Hawks. He assisted the Cup-winning goal in Game Six. The following year he led all playoff scorers with 21 points when Chicago fell to Toronto in six games.

He won his first scoring title in 1963–64, with 39 goals and 89 points, and his second in 1964–65, with 28 goals and 87 points (along with a career-high 154 PIM). In 1966–67, a new-and-improved Mikita took the NHL by storm, turning the other cheek instead of fighting every aggressor, and proving he could succeed without brawling. He won two more scoring titles (1967 and 1968), taking his second Lady Byng in 1968 as well. On October 15, 1972, he became the sixth NHLer ever to notch 1,000 career points, and on February 27, 1977, he became the eighth player in NHL history to score 500 goals. Mikita (who helped invent the banana-blade hockey stick) retired in 1980 with 541 goals and 1,467 points in 1,394 games. He entered the Hall of Fame 1983.

Dickie Moore

When he broke into the NHL with Montreal in the early 1950s, some felt Dickie Moore would be the next Rocket Richard. While that outlandish prediction was a subject of great debate, Moore proved, particularly in playoff action, that he was a player of legendary proportions. In the 1957 finals, he scored the Cup-winning goal against Boston in Game Five; in 1959 he was the playoff point leader (17) as the Habs beat Toronto in five; and in 1960 his six post-season goals led all NHLers as Montreal applied the broom to the Leafs to take its fifth straight championship.

A scrappy winger with a great shot and an unquench-able thirst for competition, Moore spent 14 seasons in the NHL—with Montreal, Toronto, and St. Louis—and announced his retirement a total of three times before it finally stuck.

Richard Winston Moore (born January 6, 1931) was a native of Montreal and played his way up through the Canadiens' minor hockey hierarchy, skating for the Junior Canadiens and the Montreal Royals before making his NHL debut at the age of 20. He split the first three seasons of his professional career (1951–54) between the NHL and the minors, and struggled to make an impact until 1956–57, when he ripped 29 goals while skating on a line with Henri and Maurice Richard.

In 1957–58, Moore emerged as a true NHL star when he captured his first Art Ross Trophy, scoring a league-high 36 goals and finishing with 84 points, four points ahead of his centerman, Henri Richard. As a follow-up, Moore proved he was no one-trick pony by winning a second straight scoring championship in 1958–59 with a career-high 41 goals, 55 assists (tops in the league), and 96 points, eclipsing Gordie Howe's single-season NHL record of 95 points, set in 1952–53. That year, he led the Canadiens to their fourth consecutive Stanley Cup and topped the list of playoff scorers with 17 points.

Often injured throughout his career, the tough, stylish winger finally quit in 1963 after a dozen NHL seasons with the Habs. However, when Toronto made him an offer to return to the ice wars in 1964–65, Moore accepted, but scored only twice in 38 games. After a second retirement, Moore made a second, far-more triumphant return in 1967–68 with the expansion St. Louis Blues, helping the first-year team go all the way to the Stanley Cup finals against Moore's old mates from Montreal. In 18 playoff games, Moore scored seven goals and 14 points, tops on the Blues, who were swept by Les Habs. The rambunctious Moore finally quit for good in 1968 with 261 goals and 608 points in 719 games, and entered the Hall of Fame in 1974.

Howie Morenz

Rocket Richard may have been the most thrilling player in Montreal's theatre of hockey entertainment, but for pure melodrama no player could match the theatrics of Howie Morenz, the "Stratford Streak," considered by many to be one of the top five players ever to grace NHL rinks. His skating speed and intensity with the puck brought fans out of their seats every time he began an offensive rush.

During a brilliant 14-year NHL career, the Ontario native won a pair of scoring titles and was voted the league's MVP three times. His Habs won three Stanley Cup championships—including the first ever in 1924.

Howarth Willam Morenz (born September 21, 1902) grew up in Mitchell (just down the road from Stratford, Ontario), and might well have spent his career with the Maple Leafs, considering the regional nature of talent-gathering of the era, but the Leafs saw no magic in Morenz during his youth hockey career. However, Habs boss Leo Dandurand got a tip on Morenz and sent a team representative to sign the young center.

Morenz made his NHL debut in 1923–24 and, playing on a line with Aurel Joliat and Billy Boucher, paid immediate and significant dividends, taking the Habs to a Stanley Cup title against Calgary of the WCHL. In Game One, Morenz scored three goals in a 6–1 trouncing, then scored the Cup-clinching goal in Game Two.

In 1927–28, Morenz won his first scoring title when he led the NHL in goals (33) and points (51), setting a new record for single-season points, and earned the Hart Trophy as the game's most valuable player. Two years later, he scored a career-high 40 goals, but finished third in the goal-scoring race behind Boston's duo of Cooney Wei-

A superb and popular player, Morenz was dubbed "the Babe Ruth of hockey."

land (43) and Dit Clapper (41). Morenz exacted a measure of revenge during the playoffs when his Habs defeated the Bruins in two final-round games, and Morenz notched the winner in Game Two. In 1930–31, Morenz led the Habs to a first-place finish and won his second Art Ross Trophy with 51 points (including 28 goals) and his second Hart Trophy. He then took the Habs to their third Stanley Cup title in 1931 with a dramatic goal in the finale against Chicago.

Traded to Chicago, then to New York, Morenz returned to the Habs in 1936–37 but suffered a fractured leg late in the season. While in the hospital, Morenz died suddenly of cardiac failure at 35, shocking the hockey world. With 270 goals and 467 points in 550 NHL games, the Stratford Streak was elected to the Hall of Fame in 1945.

Frank Nighbor

Known as much for his grace and skill as for his non-belligerent demeanor on the ice, Frank Nighbor was one of the first true superstars of the NHL at its inception in 1917. Already established in the sport, thanks to his dramatic escapades in the Pacific Coast Hockey Association, Nighbor was a member of the Stanley Cup champion Vancouver Millionaires in 1915 before returning to his native Ontario to play for the Ottawa Senators in 1917–18.

Frank Nighbor (born in 1893) grew up in eastern Canada, where his great skating and puckhandling earned him the nickname "Flying Dutchman." He traveled west

In 1916-17, scoring ace Nighbor tallied 41 goals in just 19 games.

at the age of 20 to play in the PCHA, where hockey wizard Lester Patrick was causing a stir with his new league (which was the western Canadian equivalent of the National Hockey Association) both for players and attention. Nighbor left Vancouver after winning the Stanley Cup and played for the NHA's Ottawa entry in 1915–16, sharing the league lead in goals with teammate Joe Malone (41 goals each).

A prolific scorer, Nighbor was also a masterful backchecker, feared for his deadly application of the poke check. He was fearless and determined, playing in pain a good deal of the time, absorbing tremendous physical punishment from opponents who could not match his skill, and yet never retaliating or "lowering" himself to the levels of his adversaries.

In 1919–20, his third year in the NHL, Nighbor helped the Senators to another Stanley Cup (their first since joining the NHL). In a five-game series victory over Seattle of the

PCHL, he led all goal-scorers with six tallies and tied Frank Foyston of Seattle with seven points—tops among all skaters. The Senators repeated in 1920–21, but Nighbor was held to just one goal in the playoffs.

Nighbor won the first-ever Hart Trophy as the NHL's most valuable player in 1923–24, skating on a line with Cy Denneny and Punch Broadbent, then added a pair of Lady Byng Trophies (the first two ever awarded) in 1924–25 and 1925–26. After four Stanley Cup championships with Ottawa, he moved briefly to the Toronto Maple Leafs, where he played the second half of the 1929–30 series before calling it quits. In 351 NHL games, Nighbor scored 135 goals and 197 points. Despite his natural tendency to turn the other cheek, he managed to spend 266 minutes in the penalty box during his career. When the Hockey Hall of Fame announced their very first inductees in 1945, Frank Nighbor was among them.

Bobby Orr

On May 10, 1970, Bobby Orr took a pass from Bruins center Derek Sanderson and chipped the puck past Hall of Fame goalie Glenn Hall, in the nets for the St. Louis Blues. The goal, scored 40 seconds into overtime of Game Four of the 1970 Stanley Cup Finals, gave Boston its first championship in 30 years, and catapulted Orr—a budding superstar—into his ultimate role as a full-fledged NHL hero.

That year, Orr (a fourth-year NHL pro at just 21 years of age) won his third Norris Trophy as the league's top defender and captured his first scoring title with 120 points, setting a new record for points by a defenseman. He also set a league mark for assists (87). For his tremendous effort he was voted the league's MVP, winning his first of three Hart Trophies. On top of it all, he added the Conn Smythe Trophy as the outstanding player in the Stanley Cup playoffs.

Robert Gordon Orr (born March 20, 1948) was earning accolades long before he burst upon the NHL as a 17-year-old rookie in 1966–67. A native of Parry Sound, Ontario, Orr became property of the Bruins at age 12, a function of the league's former "protected list" policy which predated the entry draft system. He began his Junior A career at Oshawa at age 13 and was a prodigy of the highest order, earning all-star status despite playing against older, bigger players. After only three years, he was ready for the NHL. Orr joined the Bruins in 1966–67 and earned the Calder Trophy as rookie of the year with 13 goals and 41 points in 61 games.

During the next dozen years, Orr played brilliantly but was plagued by crippling knee injuries. He won two scoring titles (1970 and 1975), took the Norris Trophy eight years in a row (surpassing the great Doug Harvey, who captured seven in eight years), won a pair of Stanley Cups (1970 and 1972), and took two Conn Smythe Trophies (1970 and 1972). In 1970–71, he set league records for most assists in one season by a defenseman (102) and most points in one season by a defenseman (139).

In 1976–77, after 10 years with Boston, he signed a free agent contract with Chicago. But his knees failed him, and in

Orr earned top defenseman honors a record-setting eight consecutive times.

1979, at just 30, he was forced into premature retirement. One of the most dynamic players in NHL history, Orr holds the fourth best points-per-game average of all-time (1.393), fourth all-time in goals by a defenseman (270), and sixth all-time in points by a defenseman (915). He was elected to the Hall of Fame in 1979.

Bernie Parent

The 1973–74 season was an exercise in vindication for Bernie Parent, a former Bruins prospect who went from Boston to Philadelphia and on to Toronto before finding his way back to the Flyers after a stint in the World Hockey Association. At 28, the smooth goalie from Quebec set an NHL record with 47 wins (in a 78-game schedule) and was a singular monument to grace and elegance on a Flyers team known as the Broad Street Bullies for their penchant to dominate teams and win games with intimidation and brawling.

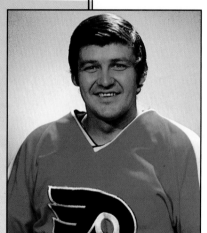

With Parent in goal, the Flyers became the first expansion team to win the Cup.

Parent, who led the NHL in '73–74 with 4,314 minutes played, also surrendered the fewest goals (136), boasted the most shutouts (12), and enjoyed the best goals-against average in the league (1.89). For his excellence, he was awarded the Vezina Trophy. But the story wasn't over. In the Stanley Cup playoffs, Parent continued to be brilliant as the Flyers swept Atlanta, narrowly edged the Rangers in seven semifinal games, and overpowered the awesome Bruins in the finals to win the first Stanley Cup in franchise history. Parent maintained a 2.02 GA average through the post-season and was named the Conn Smythe Trophy winner as MVP.

Bernard Marcel Parent (born April 3, 1945) hailed from Montreal and dreamed of growing up to play goal for the Canadiens, following in the tradition of Georges Vezina, Bill Durnan, George Hainsworth, and Jacques Plante. Bernie turned pro with the Bruins at a time when Eddie Johnston and Gerry Cheevers were already establishing themselves as bona fide NHLers. Bernie toiled in the minors, then found himself unprotected in the expansion draft of 1967, when the Flyers landed his services. He later was traded to Toronto, where he spent a year and a half before the Leafs traded him back to Philly. In the meantime, Parent had opted to take advantage of the big money being offered by WHA teams. But after one season with the Philadelphia Blazers, during which he led the league in wins (33), he jumped back to the NHL, rejoining the Flyers and enjoying his greatest NHL days.

Thanks to Parent's brilliant goaltending, his cool-under-fire demeanor, and his unflappable style, the Flyers repeated as Stanley Cup champs in 1975, beating Buffalo—and Parent became the first goalie ever to win back-to-back Vezina and Conn Smythe Trophies.

In 1978–79, an errant stick found Parent's right eye behind the mask, causing permanent damage to his retina and forcing him to retire. A two-time Stanley Cup champ, Parent was elected to the Hall of Fame in 1984.

Brad Park

Brad Park was one of the most respected backliners in hockey during his 17-year career in the 1970s and 1980s—but one thing kept him from realizing an even greater place in NHL history than he did. And that thing was Bobby Orr, who absolutely dominated the NHL as the game's most dynamic defenseman. Park was Orr's chief rival and a brilliant offensive weapon in his own right during eight years with the New York Rangers and eight more with the Bruins before he finished off his career with the Red Wings in 1985.

Nominated for the Norris Trophy as the league's top defender six times from 1970 to 1978, he finished second to Orr four times and was surpassed twice more by New York Islanders rival Denis Potvin.

Park never did capture the award itself, and thanks to Orr and Potvin, he never fulfilled his foremost ambition—to win a Stanley Cup. The Bruins—with Orr at the controls—eliminated Park's Rangers from the playoffs in 1970 and 1972 (in the finals, no less), while Potvin's Islanders shocked the Rangers in 1975 in the first round, a crushing defeat that spelled the end of an era and brought on a major retooling of the Rangers' lineup. The following year, during the 1975–76 season, Park was traded to the Bruins for Phil Esposito, a deal that astonished fans up and down Interstate 95 between Manhattan and Boston.

Douglas Bradford Park (born July 6, 1948) was raised in Toronto and played his Junior A hockey with the

Although the Stanley Cup eluded him, Park was a seven-time All-Star.

fabled Toronto Marlies of the Ontario league. After a sterling junior career, many thought he would ultimately graduate to the Maple Leafs, but the newly instituted entry draft allowed the Rangers to acquire his rights. An impressive training camp in 1968 earned him a spot on Broadway. A terrific two-way player, Park scored more than 20 goals three times (24, 25, and 22) and six times banged his way to more than 100 penalty minutes. Nobody threw a better hip check than Park, and few defenders could command a power play or conduct the transition from defense to offense (and back) with more skill, grace, and alacrity.

After notching 378 points in 465 games for the Rangers, and another 417 points in 501 games for the Bruins, Park ultimately finished his career with the Red Wings, accumulating 101 points in 147 games before hanging up his skates at the end of the 1984–85 season. He was elected to the Hall of Fame in 1988.

Gilbert Perreault

In the old days of protected lists and team-owned junior programs, Gilbert Perreault would have become a Montreal Canadien player by the very nature of his pre-NHL career, during which he competed for the Montreal Junior Canadiens of the OHA. But instead of carving his name into the NHL's history books with an established NHL power, it was Perreault's fate to become the first player ever drafted by the Buffalo Sabres, an expansion team that entered the league in the fall of 1970. Perreault, the first player chosen overall in the '70 amateur draft, was coming off an MVP year in juniors, having just scored 51 goals and 121 points in 54 games for his league-champion team (despite being beaten in the OHA scoring race by St. Catherines center Marcel Dionne).

In his first NHL season, the stocky speed-merchant with the blistering shot and limitless array of moves banged home 38 goals and 72 points in 78 games and was named the 1971 rookie of the year, winning the Calder Trophy in a heated contest with Minnesota's Jude Drouin.

Gilbert Perreault (born November 13, 1950) was raised in Victoriaville, Quebec, a sub-

Perreault holds Sabres team records for games, goals, points, and assists.

urb of Montreal, where he grew up watching some of the greatest teams in Canadiens history. In his last two years of junior hockey at Montreal, he ripped 88 goals and 218 points in just 108 games. If he was disappointed at going to Buffalo, a struggling new team, instead of the Habs, he never let it show in his game.

A dynamic skater with great acceleration and master-ful puck control, Perreault ultimately became the center of the Sabres' fabled "French Connection Line" with Richard Martin on the left wing and Rene Robert on the right. His combination of finesse, high scoring, and gentlemanly play earned him the Lady Byng Trophy in 1973. In 1974–75, the Sabres went all the way to the Stanley Cup finals on the strength of the French Connection Line, though they ultimately lost to the Flyers. Perreault's line accounted for 131 goals and 291 points. In 1975–76, Perreault reached personal career highs in goals (44), assists (69), and points (113), finishing third in the league scoring race.

On March 9, 1986, Perreault became the 12th man in NHL history to score 500 career goals. Though he never won a Stanley Cup during his 17 pro seasons, Perreault retired with a career point-per-game average of 1.11 (1,326 points in 1,191 games). He was elected to the Hall of Fame in 1990.

Pierre Pilote

Without their brilliant defenseman Pierre Pilote on the backline in the 1961 Stanley Cup playoffs, it's conceivable the Chicago Blackhawks would not have beaten the Detroit Red Wings to capture their third playoff championship. Pilote, a crafty puckhandler with a healthy mean streak, led all post-season scorers with 12 assists—and half of those came in the finals alone. Blessed with the ability to step up in crucial situations, he set up Bobby Hull's game-winning goal in Game One, assisted Ron Murphy's winner in Game Three, and earned the first assist on Stan Mikita's clincher in Game Five. He finished the playoffs tied with Gordie Howe for the overall lead in points (15). Had there been such an award at the time, Pilote would surely have been a candidate for playoff MVP honors.

Pierre Paul Pilote (born December 11, 1931) grew up in Quebec and seemed on his way to the typical junior career when the local ice hockey arena burned to the ground, leaving him and his mates without a place to skate. Luckily, he was spotted by the coach of St. Catherines, Rudy Pilous, who worked under the auspices of the Blackhawks. After several seasons in the minors, Pierre made it to the NHL in 1955–56 with 20 games in a Chicago sweater. He never played another game on the farm.

In 1962–63, two years after helping the 'Hawks to their third (and last) Stanley Cup victory, Pilote was named the NHL's top defenseman, earning the Norris Trophy for the first of three straight years. Though his scoring was modest by modern standards, he demonstrated such a complete panoply of skills—from moving the puck out of his own zone to physically manhandling any opponents who lingered too long near his goalie—that there was no defenseman in the league who could compare to him.

In 1964–65, when he captured his final Norris Trophy, Pilote reached a career high in goals (14) and points (59) and came within three minutes of tying his personal high for penalty minutes, sitting out 162 PIM.

Following the 1967–68 season, his 13th in Chicago, Pilote was traded to Toronto for an up-and-coming winger named Jim Pappin, who went on to enjoy an illustrious career with the 'Hawks. Pierre, then 37 years old, saw the writing on the wall. After a three-goal, 21-point performance in 69 games in Toronto, Pilote called it quits after the 1968–69 season with 890 NHL games to his credit.

One of the most respected two-way defensemen of his era, Pilote was elected to the Hall of Fame in 1975.

Pilote took the coveted James Norris Trophy in 1963, '64, and '65.

Jacques Plante

Though he was known far and wide for his fiercely emotional engagement during games, Jacques Plante was one of the most intelligent, cerebral, and analytical men the NHL has ever seen—a trendsetter and a trail-blazer throughout his brilliant 19-year career. Perhaps most famous for introducing the face mask into normal goalie equipment (thanks to a multitude of injuries), he revolutionized the very art of goaltending by being the first netminder regularly to leave the crease, handle the puck, and become involved in the transition from defense to offense. Such modern-day goalies as Ron Hextall and Ed Belfour owe much to Plante's inventiveness.

Plante wasn't just smart, however. He was also one of the most talented puckstoppers ever to grace NHL arenas. During 11 seasons with Montreal, he won six Stanley Cups (1953, 1956–60) and earned six Vezina Trophies of his own (1956–60 and 1962) and later shared one with Glenn Hall in St. Louis (1969). Skating for Montreal, the Rangers, St. Louis, Toronto, and Edmonton of the WHA, "Jake the Snake" suited up for 837 NHL games and amassed 434 wins, second only to Terry Sawchuk (435) on the all-time list. His 82 career shutouts rank fourth all-time.

Joseph Jacques Plante (born January 17, 1929) was the oldest of 11 children growing up on a farm in Mount Carmel, Quebec (and later in Shawinigan), without many privileges or excesses. At six, he began playing hockey, but an asthmatic condition made skating a hazard, so he settled on goaltending. By 14 he was playing against 18-year-olds; by 18 he was a star of the Quebec Citadels. During his brief career in the Quebec Senior Hockey League, he often func-tioned as practice goalie for the Canadiens, who owned his NHL rights. He played three regular season games with the Habs and four more in the playoffs and got his name on the 1953 Stanley Cup.

In 1953–54, Plante officially turned pro and split the year between the AHL and NHL. By 1954–55, he had replaced Gerry McNeil as the Habs' starting goalie and, in his first full NHL season, led the league in wins (31). He then followed up with a league-high 42 wins in 1955–56, along with the lowest goals-against average in the league (1.86)—good enough to earn him his first of seven Vezina Trophies.

In 1961–62, Plante matched his career high with 42 wins, led the NHL in GA average (2.37), won his sixth Vezina, and earned MVP honors with a Hart Trophy. Though his game gradually faded between 1963 (when he was traded to New York) and 1975 (when he retired), he deservedly gained Hall of Fame recognition in 1978.

Denis Potvin

The ultimate "franchise" player, Denis Potvin was the first player picked in the 1973 amateur draft, chosen by the New York Islanders (who'd only been in existence one year before Potvin's arrival). A rugged defenseman who could dominate physically as well as carry the offensive attack on his shoulders, Potvin was the cornerstone of an organization that grew into a bona fide dynasty.

In 1973–74, following an often brilliant junior career, Potvin joined the Isles and immediately established himself with 54 points and 175 PIM. He beat Atlanta's Tom Lysiak for rookie honors, taking the 1974 Calder Trophy. In 1974–75, he made the First All-Star Team—the first of five such honors—and guided the Isles to their first playoff berth. After shocking the Rangers in the opening round, they upset Pittsburgh in seven games and extended the Flyers to a seventh game before falling.

Denis Charles Potvin (born Octber 29, 1953) grew up in Ottawa, one of two hockey-playing brothers to skate in the NHL (older brother Jean skated for Los Angeles, Minnesota, Philadelphia, the Isles, and Cleveland during an 11-year career). Denis began his Junior A career at 15 with the

A leader and mentor, Potvin captained the Islanders from 1979 until 1987.

Ottawa 67s, and during the next five years he evolved from a 37-point rookie to a 123-point NHL "sure thing."

By the end of the 1975–76 season, he had established himself as the NHL's top defenseman, winning the first of three Norris Trophies. His 31 goals and 98 points, combined with 100 penalty minutes, earned him the reputation of another Bobby Orr—only with a mean streak.

No backliner in the game could do as many things as effectively as Potvin. In 1978–79, Potvin had his greatest year and suffered his greatest disappointment. Though he matched his career high for goals (31) and topped the 100-point plateau for the only time in his career—and won his third Norris Trophy in four years—his Isles were upset in the playoffs by the Rangers. It wasn't until the following year that the Islanders won their first of four straight Stanley Cups (beating the Flyers in 1980, the North Stars in 1981, the Canucks in 1982, and the Oilers in 1983).

Potvin retired at the end of the 1987-88 season. At the time, he was first all-time in goals (310), assists (742), and points (1,052) by a defenseman—and the first NHL defenseman to reach the 1,000-point plateau. His leadership, his smarts, his physical strength, and his talent made him an easy pick for the Hall of Fame, which he entered in 1991.

Babe Pratt

On April 22, 1945, the Maple Leafs and Red Wings were engaged in a pitched battle for the Stanley Cup. It was Game Seven and the score was tied 1–1 late in the third period. Tied, that is, until Toronto defender Babe Pratt took a pass from Neil Metz and fired the puck past Harry Lumley to give the Leafs a 2–1 lead. Toronto staved off Detroit's finest last-gasp efforts and captured the Cup, its fifth championship. Pratt, who had earlier helped the Rangers win the 1940 Cup, scored only two goals during that playoff season, but he sure knew how to make them count.

Walter "Babe" Pratt (born January 7, 1916) was born in rural Manitoba but grew up in Winnipeg, where he played hockey on frozen outdoor rinks. He eventually earned the respect and admiration of NHL scouts not only with his great size (6'3" and 210 pounds) but also with his great two-way play. Pratt was as quick to deliver a stand-up open-ice bodycheck as to skate the

puck the length of the ice and shoot on goal. In 1935, he signed with Lester Patrick to play for the Rangers. As a sophomore in 1936–37, he finished second among NHL defensemen in goals (eight).

Pratt earned his first Stanley Cup championship in 1940 when the Rangers beat Toronto in six games. During ensuing seasons, boss Lester Patrick developed the notion that Pratt's best years were behind him. In 1942, in one of the worst trades in Rangers history, the Blueshirts acquired defenseman Dudley "Red" Garrett and winger Hank Goldup from Toronto in exchange for the flamboyant Pratt, who was clearly not over the hill.

In 1943–44, he made Patrick look foolish when he scored 17 goals and a career-high 57 points—tops among NHL defensemen—and was

The Babe captured a pair of Stanley Cups—one with the Rangers, another with Toronto.

voted the NHL's most valuable player, garnering the Hart Trophy. The following year, he scored a career-high 18 goals and posted 41 points. Detroit's Frank "Flash" Hollett scored 20 goals and 41 points that year as Pratt's chief rival. But Pratt had the last laugh in the playoffs when his Maple Leafs pulled a six-game upset over the Habs in the first round, then beat Detroit in seven games on Pratt's Stanley Cup-winning goal in the 13th minute of the third period.

Pratt finished his NHL career in 1946–47 with Boston, having notched 83 goals and 292 points in 517 games. The two-time Stanley Cup champion bounced around the minor leagues for several more years before hanging up his skates in 1952, at the age of 36. He was elected to the Hall of Fame in 1966.

Joe Primeau

One of the great playmaking centers of his era, "Gentleman Joe" Primeau was the first man to capitalize on the NHL's rule change in 1927–28 allowing forward passes in the offensive zone. With the help of his brilliant linemates, Charlie Conacher and Busher Jackson, the little Leaf pivot quickly established himself as one of the game's most resourceful relay men. Three times in his illustrious but all-too-brief nine-year career, he led the NHL in assists. In 1930–31, he counted 32 helpers among his 41 points; in 1931–32, he reached a career high with 37 assists and 50 points; and in 1933–34, he set up 32 goals and posted 46 total points.

In 1931–32, Toronto's fabled "Kid Line" captured hockey's unofficial triple crown. Center Primeau led the league in assists (37), right winger Charlie Conacher led in goals (34)—tying Ranger Bill Cook—and left winger Busher Jackson captured the league scoring title with 53 points.

While Jackson took the Ross Trophy, Primeau took the Lady Byng Trophy for his combined skill and clean play.

Primeau's line did its most damage and enjoyed its greatest results that same year, eliminating the Montreal Maroons, four goals to three, in the first round of playoffs, then sweeping the Rangers in three straight games to capture the 1932 Stanley Cup. Primeau, ever the vital assist man, tied Frank Boucher of the Rangers with six assists to lead all post-season scorers.

Joseph Primeau (born January 29, 1906) was raised in Ontario. Slight of build, he was not one of the NHL's top prospects in the province during his junior hockey career. But he did catch the eye of Frank Selke, Jr., a brilliant talent judge, who suggested to Maple Leaf boss Conn Smythe that Primeau had the right stuff. After two brief tastes of NHL action, Primeau finally made the Leafs' roster in 1929–30. After he was united with Conacher and Jackson,

the history books had to be rewritten.

Primeau finished his NHL career in 1936, having notched 66 goals and 243 points in 310 games. His decision to leave the game at just 30 years of age came as a shock to many who felt he still had plenty of quality hockey left in him. But just as Primeau had never let his diminutive physique lessen his competitiveness or effectiveness, he was not about to let his mind be changed by the desires of others. Following Primeau's retirement, the team went through an understandable period of struggle. For his outstanding play and sportsmanship, Primeau was elected to the Hall of Fame in 1963.

The "Kid Line" of (L-R) Conacher, Primeau, and Jackson won it all in 1931–32.

Marcel Pronovost

There may have been many defensemen in the long history of the NHL with more offensive talent, more grace, and perhaps even more style than Marcel Pronovost. But never has a tougher man pulled on an NHL sweater and skated out onto the frozen battlefield with more courage or indifference for personal safety than this veteran who starred in Detroit and Toronto over a 20-year career.

Rene Marcel Pronovost (born June 15, 1930) was raised in Quebec, where he played junior hockey at Shawinigan Falls until a Red Wings scout found him. At just 15, he was signed to a minor pro contract. In 1949, playing in Omaha, he was named the USHL's rookie of the year. When injuries carved into the Red Wings roster during the 1950 playoffs (specifically, a near fatal head injury to Gordie Howe), Pronovost was called up on an emergency fill-in basis to bolster the lineup. He played admirably, earning his name on the 1950 Stanley Cup—a feat he would repeat four times during his career.

Pronovost arrived at Red Wings camp in the fall of 1950, fresh from his superb playoff showing, ready to earn a steady NHL job. But a fractured cheek cost him that opportunity, and he spent half the year on the farm before eventually finishing his rookie year (1950–51) with the Wings. Over the next 14 seasons, Pronovost became a key member of the Detroit defense corps, using his strength and savvy in equal measure. His disregard for his personal safety resulted in hundreds of stitches, broken bones, and

Both fearless and tireless, Pronovost skated for five Cup-winning teams.

other nagging injuries—yet he never changed his style.

Though he played somewhat in the shadow of Red Kelly, Pronovost helped the Red Wings to three more Stanley Cups (1952, 1954, and 1955), and set up Gordie Howe's Cup-clinching goal in Game Seven of the 1955 finals against Montreal.

Just a month before his 35th birthday, following the 1964–65 season, Pronovost was traded to Toronto in an eight-player deal that resulted in Andy Bathgate transferring from the Leafs to Detroit. Pronovost played four more seasons with the Maple Leafs, and put his name onto a fifth Stanley Cup in 1967. At 39, after playing seven games of the 1969–70 season, Pronovost called it quits. He finished with 88 goals, 345 points, and 821 penalty minutes in 1,206 regular season games—plus a dozen more goals and 37 points in 134 playoff games. A First-Team All-Star in 1960 and1961, Pronovost entered the Hall of Fame in 1978.

Jean Ratelle

One of the most graceful and gentlemanly players ever to lace up skates in the NHL, Jean Ratelle also experienced the shock of being part of one of the most dramatic and stunning trades in the history of the New York Rangers and Boston Bruins.

On November 7, 1975, after 15 years on Broadway, Ratelle, a longtime fan favorite at Madison Square Garden, was shipped (along with All-Star defenseman Brad Park) to the Bruins in exchange for future Hall of Famer Phil Esposito, whose dislike of New York (the city, its fans, and its hockey team) was surpassed only by the hatred Rangers fans held for him. For his part, Ratelle made the transition to Beantown with his usual grace, continuing to chalk up big numbers and helping the Bruins remain a contender for the Stanley Cup, though he never did sip from the cherished silver goblet.

Joseph Gilbert Yvon Jean Ratelle (born October 3, 1940), who apprenticed for the NHL in the Quebec juniors before signing with the Rangers in 1960, was a "poor man's" Jean Beliveau—a hero of Quebec junior hockey before turning pro. He also showed tremendous courage and perseverance early in his career when he recovered from spinal fusion surgery (which was necessary to repair damaged disks in his back) when he was still in his early 20s.

Playing with Rod Gilbert and Vic Hadfield during most of his Rangers career, Ratelle was the pivotman on the "GAG Line," which stood for "Goal-a-Game." In 1971–72, when the Rangers were among the favorites to win the Stanley Cup, Ratelle had his greatest season—scoring 46 goals and 109 points while sitting out just four minutes in penalties. That he missed 15 games with a broken ankle made the accomplishment even more spectacular. For his superb performance he won the Lady Byng Trophy for skill and sportsmanship. Ironically, he won the award for a second time in 1975–76 when he split the year between New York and Boston. Despite the traumatic change of scenery that year, he tallied 38 goals and 105 points (with just 18 PIM).

On April 3, 1977, in a 7–4 home-ice victory over Toronto, Ratelle notched an assist to record his 1,000th career point, making him the 12th man in NHL history to reach that plateau. He finished his 21-year NHL career in 1981 with 491 goals and 1,267 points in 1,281 games. Though he never won a Stanley Cup, he was deservedly elected to the Hall of Fame in 1985.

"Gentleman Jean" recorded 20 or more goals for 14 straight seasons.

Henri Richard

In 20 NHL seasons with the Montreal Canadiens, Henri "The Pocket Rocket" Richard enjoyed 18 trips to the Stanley Cup playoffs and, in those 18 playoff appearances, partook of no fewer than 11 titles. And he was typically a major contributor.

On May 5, 1966, during the championship round between Montreal and the Red Wings, Richard knocked the puck past Detroit goalie Roger Crozier two and a half minutes into sudden death overtime of Game Six to give the Habs the Stanley Cup, their 13th such championship. Richard, who led all playoff scorers in 1960, notched only one goal in the 1966 post-season—but it was a huge goal.

Joseph Henri Richard (born February 29, 1936) arrived on the NHL scene in 1955 after his big brother, the legendary Maurice "Rocket" Richard, had been a dominating force for more than a decade. Initially considered to be a longshot for immediate entry to the NHL—he was just

19—little Henri, who stood just 5'7" and 160 pounds, set about proving he belonged in the NHL on his own merits, not just as the kid brother to a living hero. He scored 19 rookie goals in 1955–56. In his third pro season, 1957–58, playing on a line with his brother, Henri led the NHL in assists (52) and enjoyed a career-high 80 points.

In 1970–71, Richard crafted another gigantic moment in the history of the Habs' amazing Stanley Cup excellence. During the seventh game of the finals, this time against Chicago and a brick wall of a goalie named Tony Esposito, Richard again delivered a crucial goal when he converted a pass from winger Rejean Houle and unlocked a 2–2 game early in the third period with his fifth tally of the playoffs. The goal stood up as Montreal goalie Ken Dryden turned away the Blackhawks' best efforts during the game's final 17 minutes. (Richard stands as one of only eight NHLers to notch more than one Stanley

Cup-winning goal—the others including Jack Darragh, Howie Morenz, Toe Blake, Jean Beliveau, Bobby Orr, Jacques Lemaire, and Mike Bossy.)

Though he never won a scoring title, he finished second overall in 1958 and fourth overall in 1960 and 1963. On December 20, 1973, during a 2–2 tie in Buffalo, Richard posted an assist that counted for his 1,000th career point. After the 1973–74 season, he added the Masterton Trophy (for dedication) to his impressive resume. He went on to finish his 20-year career with 1,046 points in 1,256 games before retiring after the 1974–75 season. He entered the Hall of Fame in 1979.

Richard played for 20 seasons with Montreal, winning 11 Stanley Cups.

Maurice Richard

In the history of the National Hockey League, perhaps no player personified the Jekyll and Hyde dual-personality more than Maurice "Rocket" Richard. During his nearly two decades in the NHL, from the early 1940s until his retirement in 1960, Richard was Montreal's fire-breathing leader on the ice, an intense competitor who would skate through a wall to score a goal. At the same time, however, he was shy and reserved—a veritable teddy bear—away from the rink.

Not satisfied to be simply the best he could be, Richard strived to be the best in the game—a trailblazer and a record-setter. He was the first man ever to score 50 goals in a season, an accomplishment considered by many to be impossible. And Richard not only reached the 50-goal plateau, he did it in only 50 games. On March 18, 1945, in the final game of the 1944–45 regular season, 23-year-old Richard beat Boston goalie Harvey Bennett in a 4–2 win at Boston Garden and etched his name in the history books. Though others followed Richard in reaching the 50-goal plateau, his 50-goals-in-50-games masterpiece remained an untouchable record for 37 years, until a 20-year-old phenom named Wayne Gretzky scored 50 goals in only 39 games during the 1981–82 season. (Earlier, during the 1980–81 campaign, New York Islander right winger Mike Bossy, a hard-shooting sniper in his own right, had equaled Richard's mark when he notched his 50th goal of the year in his 50th game, against Quebec, on his way to a 68-goal season.)

During his 18-year NHL career with the Canadiens, Richard went to the playoffs 15 times and helped the Habs to eight Stanley Cup titles, including five in a row from 1955 to 1960.

Richard was a dominating offensive weapon, leading the NHL in goals five times

A terror on the ice, Richard was gentle and soft-spoken away from the rink.

(1944–45, 1946–47, 1949–50, 1953–54, and 1954–55) and capturing the Hart Trophy as the NHL's most valuable player in 1946–47 when he ripped 45 goals. On the evening of October 19, 1957, in a 3–1 victory over the visiting Chicago Blackhawks, Richard scored against future Hall of Fame goalie Glenn Hall. It was the 500th goal of his career, making him the first player in NHL history to reach that plateau.

Joseph Henri Maurice Richard (born August 4, 1921) was destined to play for the Canadiens. Born and raised in Montreal, Richard caught the

eye of scouts early on with his quick-footed, unpredictable style. It was soon noted that Richard's otherwise mild-mannered temperament would vanish the moment his skates touched the ice; his placid expression would turn icy and tenacious; his eyes would burn with determination. Clever and creative, he relied upon an assortment of fakes and full-bore attacks to beat defenders

and goalies, seemingly without ever repeating himself.

A skilled baseball player and boxer, Richard had tremendous athletic ability and acute hand-eye coordination, which helped him immensely with his first love: hockey. Though he continued to excel as a multisport teenage athlete, it was clear that a career in the NHL was his providence. In 1942, at the

Intensely competitive with a fiery temper, the Rocket racked up 1,285 career penalty minutes.

age of 21, Richard turned pro with Montreal, but his first NHL season was a near disaster, plagued by injuries that limited him to just 16 games. However, as a sophomore in 1943–44, playing on the fabled "Punch Line" with Elmer Lach and Toe Blake, Richard scored 32 goals and proved he had the right stuff for the NHL. On December 28, 1944, Richard entered the record books for the first time when he registered eight points in a single game. While the Canadiens were handing Detroit a humiliating 9–1 thrashing at the Forum, Richard was a one-man wrecking crew, scoring five goals against Harry Lumley, and adding three assists.

Despite his devastating goal-scoring talent, Richard never won a league scoring title. He finished in the top five nine times, including five second-place finishes and a pair of third-place finishes. He came close to winning the Art Ross Trophy in 1946–47 when he notched 71 points and finished just one point behind Chicago's Max Bentley.

In 1954–55, he seemed to have his first scoring title locked up when violence and controversy derailed his efforts. Leading Montreal teammate Bernie "Boom Boom" Geoffrion by a handful of points with just three games

To honor his greatness, the Habs retired Richard's number (9) in 1960.

to go in the season, Richard became embroiled in a nasty stick fight with Boston's Hal Laycoe that captured the attention and disgust of NHL president Clarence Campbell. Despite his celebrity status and his apparent appointment with a long-awaited scoring championship, the Rocket was suspended for the rest of the season—and the playoffs!—by Campbell. A riot broke out in the Montreal Forum during the team's next home game and Campbell was assaulted by angry fans. During his suspension, Richard was caught and passed by Geoffrion, who won the scoring title with 75 points to the Rocket's 74. For his trou-

ble, Geoffrion became the target of venom and wrath among Canadien fans who wanted Richard to win the coveted title. Richard never came so close again, but the greatness of his career was in no way diminished by this single "failure."

It was Richard's ferocious nature on the ice that helped define the firewagon style of hockey that made Montreal both dangerous and successful. There was no greater "clutch" player than the Rocket, who scored 82 goals in 133 playoff games, including the Cup-winner in 1956. His half-dozen sudden death overtime goals still stand as the all-time record, demonstrating both his flair for the dramatic and his immeasurable value when the game was on the line.

Richard hung up his skates at the end of the 1959–60 season, at the age of 39, with 544 career goals. Had he played one more season, he might have become the first player to reach the 1,000-point mark. But Richard knew when his time was up, so he quit with 965 points in 978 games and watched as Gordie Howe reached the millennium during the 1960–61 season, Richard's first year of retirement. The Rocket went into the Hall of Fame in 1961.

Larry Robinson

Though he scored nearly 600 fewer goals in his NHL career, Larry Robinson shares a significant record with the legendary Gordie Howe: 20 years in the Stanley Cup playoffs. Robinson stands alone with 20 straight appearances in the post-season, starting in his rookie year with Montreal (1972–73) and ending with the Kings (1991–92). With 227 playoff games to his credit, Robinson is the most experienced playoff performer in NHL history. During his 17-year career with the Habs, he put his name on six Stanley Cups, including four straight from 1976 to 1979.

A big (6′4″, 225 pounds), rangy defenseman with great toughness, intelligence, and playmaking skill, Robinson was a decorated warrior, winning a pair of Norris Trophies as the game's top defender. He also earned the Conn Smythe Trophy as MVP of the 1978 Stanley Cup playoffs, when he led all scorers in assists (17) and tied teammate Guy Lafleur in total points (21).

Laurence Clark Robinson (born June 2, 1951) hailed from Winchester, Ontario, and played his junior hockey at Brockville and Kitchener before he was drafted 20th in the 1971 amateur draft. The

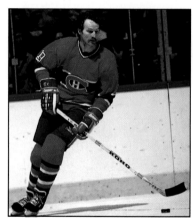

Robinson ranks third all-time in assists by a defenseman (750).

Habs sent Robinson to Nova Scotia for parts of two seasons before making him a permanent fixture on the backline in Montreal, where Forum fans quickly took a liking to his physical toughness and puck-handling skill.

In 1976–77, he scored 19 goals and 85 points and earned his first Norris Trophy, a feat he would repeat three years later, in 1979–80, with a 75-point performance.

In the 1976 playoffs, Robinson showed another side when his Habs challenged the two-time Stanley Cup champion Philadelphia Flyers in the finals. The Broad Street Bullies had dominated with intimidation and skill, but when Robinson took on Dave "Hammer" Schultz and decisively thrashed the Flyers' chief pugilist, the Habs developed the necessary courage, and ultimately swept the defending champs and won the next three titles (from 1976 to 1979).

After playing out his contract with Montreal in 1989, Robinson signed on as a free agent in Los Angeles, where he played for three years before calling it quits after the 1991–92 season. He finished his 20-year NHL career with 208 goals and 958 points in 1,384 games. In 1994–95, he won another Cup with the New Jersey Devils as assistant coach.

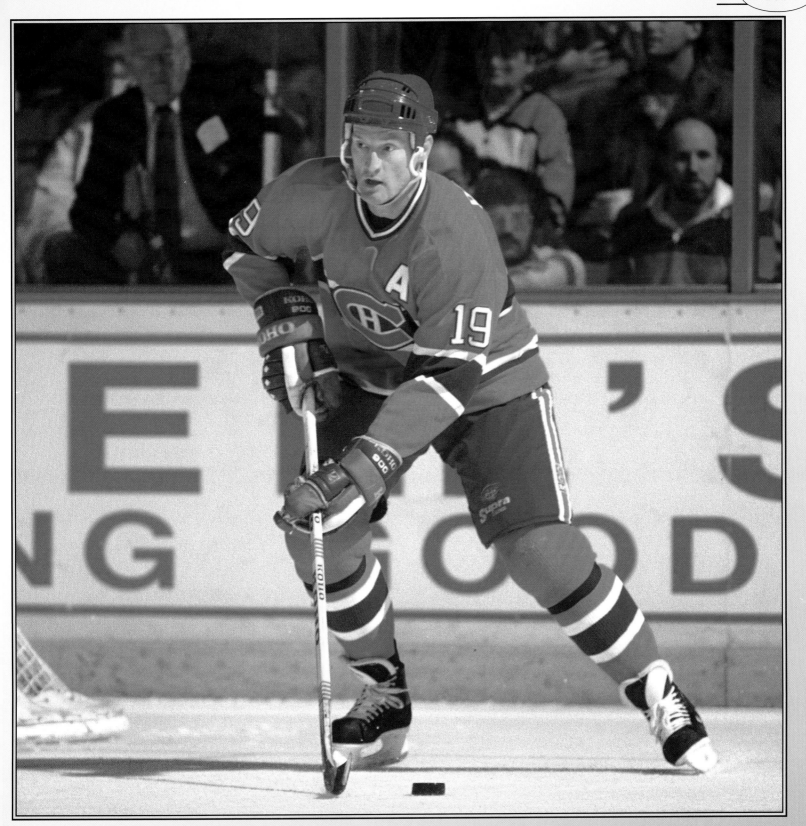

Luc Robitaille

When the Los Angeles Kings selected Luc Robitaille 171st in the 1984 entry draft (170 picks after Mario Lemieux went first overall), precious few hockey watchers gave the Montreal native much of a chance to make the NHL. He was a terrible skater by NHL standards; too slow, not physical enough, and worst of all, lethargic in his approach to defensive hockey—a curse of many Quebec junior leaguers.

During the next two years, Robitaille put his nose to the proverbial grindstone and became simply the best player in junior hockey. In 127 games covering two seasons, he notched 123 goals and 340 points and was named the Canadian Major Junior Player of the Year for 1985–86. He joined the Kings in 1986–87 and scored 45 goals and 84 points to win the Calder Trophy as rookie of the year. Not only did he prove he was no fluke, but he then shrugged off a sophomore jinx by ripping 53 goals and 111 points in his second NHL season.

Luc Robitaille (born February 17, 1966) proved that first impressions aren't always the best ones as he grew from a less-than-spectacular freshman winger at Hull in the Quebec junior league to a bona fide superstar in the NHL by the time he was 21 years old.

In 1992–93, his seventh year in the league, Robitaille set a pair of NHL records when he scored 63 goals and notched 125 points, the most ever by a left winger in both categories. He also came within sniffing range of a Stanley Cup when his Kings skated into the finals against Montreal, only to lose in five games (three of those losses coming in heartbreaking sudden-death overtime).

Robitaille's tenure with the Kings extended over eight seasons (1986–94) and included goal totals of 45, 53, 46, 52, 45, 44, 63, and 44. Four times he amassed more than 100 points (111, 101, 107, and 125) and had an impressive 1.25 points-per-game average after 640 NHL contests.

On July 29, 1994, he was traded to Pittsburgh for bang-and-crash right winger Rick Tocchet in a move some have suggested was devised by Kings superstar Wayne Gretzky, with whom Robitaille reputedly had maintained a cool rapport. If he was irked by his transfer, the hard-skating left winger showed no sign of it. In just 46 games he scored 23 goals (including No. 400 of his career) and 42 points. Barring a catastrophic injury, Robitaille should be a sure thing for the Hall of Fame when he hangs up the skates.

Robitaille scored 40-plus goals in each of his eight seasons with the Kings.

Patrick Roy

Since its inception 30 years ago, only eight goalies have ever won the Conn Smythe Trophy as the MVP of the Stanley Cup playoffs. Only two goalies have won the trophy twice: Bernie Parent in 1974 and 1975 with Philadelphia, and Montreal's Patrick Roy, first as a rookie in 1986, and again in 1993.

Roy made one of the most spectacular NHL debuts in recent memory when he joined the Habs in 1985–86. Though his regular season stats were adequate by rookie standards (23–18–3 in 47 games with a 3.35 goals-against average), he was absolutely brilliant in the playoffs. He won 15 games to lead all goalies and boasted a 1.92 GA average. At just 20, he carried the Canadiens to their 23rd Stanley Cup title and won the Conn Smythe Trophy.

Patrick Roy (born October 5, 1965) was destined to play for the Canadiens, growing up in Quebec City, though he wasn't the kind of awe-inspiring performer as a youth that guaranteed stardom in the

NHL. During his three-year career at Granby in the high-scoring Quebec junior league, he saw a lot of rubber—and missed a fair amount as well—and was only the 51st player selected in the 1984 draft. However, once he got to the NHL, where Montreal had a stringent defensive style in place, Roy truly emerged.

In the years between his glorious rookie playoff performance and his next appearance in the Cup finals, Roy set about establishing himself as one of the game's great puck-stoppers. In 1986–87, he shared the William Jennings Trophy with teammate Brian Hayward for the first of three straight years, as the goalies on the NHL team that allowed the fewest goals. In 1988–89, Roy won his first GA average title with a 2.47 mark—good enough to earn him his first Vezina Trophy. He held the title the following year as well when he finished the 1989–90 season with a league-high 31 victories (with only 16 defeats) and a 2.53 GA average. In

1991–92, Roy played in 67 games for the Habs and led the league with five shutouts and a 2.36 GA average, winning him his third Vezina Trophy.

In the 1993 playoffs, Roy survived the most intense pressure imaginable, winning

Roy's quick reflexes have earned him two Stanley Cup rings

10 games in sudden death overtime—including three in the finals against Los Angeles. The Habs ultimately beat the Kings in five games to win Stanley Cup number 24—and 16-game winner Roy earned his second Conn Smythe Trophy.

In December of 1995, after 10 years with the Habs, Roy was traded to Colorado.

Borje Salming

Though he never set out to be a trailblazer, Borje Salming spent 17 years in the NHL and almost single-handedly disproved the North American theory that players from Sweden could not compete in the NHL. Salming, a graceful defenseman who played most of his career in the shadows of Bobby Orr, Denis Potvin, Ray Bourque, and Paul Coffey, not only survived in the rugged NHL, he did so in Toronto, where late Maple Leafs owner Harold Ballard was one of the harshest critics of European skaters. But Salming was as tough as he was talented, and he was skilled enough to play 1,148 games and amass 787 points and 1,344 penalty minutes.

Salming leads all Maple Leafs in assists, collecting 620 with the club.

Anders Borje Salming (born April 17, 1951) hailed from Kiruna, Sweden, and played in the demanding Swedish senior league for three years with the highly respected Brynas club. At 21, after being scouted by Toronto executives, he signed a free agent contract with the Leafs and—along with slick winger Inge Hammarstrom—journeyed to Canada to begin his NHL career.

After a tentative rookie season in 1973–74, Salming put together a string of six straight years (1974–80) when he was named either a First or Second Team All-Star. In 1976–77 he notched a career-high 78 points in 76 games and earned his only First-All-Star Team berth. In 1979–80, he scored a career-high 19 goals.

In 1985–86, Salming suffered a gruesome facial injury when he was accidentally kicked by another player in a goalmouth scramble. More than 100 stitches were needed to close the gash that ran from his forehead, between his

eyes, across the bridge of his nose, and into one cheek. If anyone had ever doubted Salming's courage, those doubts were permanently put to rest when the stylish Swede returned to action with only the addition of a plexiglass face shield on his helmet as further protection.

Salming, who graced the NHL with a complete game of technical skill, great intelligence and execution, and no small measure of toughness, finished his Toronto career in 1989 and played part of one season with Detroit in 1989–90 before calling it quits. Though he never won a major league award and never sipped champagne from the Stanley Cup, Salming played a vital role in the development of the NHL by helping to open the doors for all Europeans—not only Swedes—to compete in the league. Though some conservative North Americans still bemoan the "internationalization" of the NHL, Salming deservedly earned his place in hockey history.

Denis Savard

Few NHLers have provided more nightly thrills than Denis Savard, a highly skilled skater and puckhandler. "Savvy" is one of the NHL's most productive skaters, several times surpassing the 40-goal plateau and five times accumulating more than 100 points.

Denis Joseph Savard (born February 4, 1961) was raised in Quebec and played his junior hockey at Montreal with the Junior Canadiens. Hopeful of being drafted by the Habs, Savard put together two masterful pre-NHL seasons with 109 goals and 339 points in 142 games. He led the QMJHL in assists (112) in 1978–79. But when the Canadiens exercised their right to pick first overall in 1980, it was Doug Wicken-heiser (the Canadian Major Junior Player of the Year) who was the top pick. After Winnipeg selected Dave Babych, the Blackhawks called the name of a disappointed Savard.

After posting 75 points in 76 rookie games in 1980–81, Savard began a vigorous campaign to prove Montreal had erred in ignoring him. As a sophomore in 1981–82, he ripped 32 goals, added a career-high 87 assists, and finished with 119 points. He then upped the ante the following year with 35 goals and 121 points. His streak of 100-point seasons was interrupted in 1983–84 when injuries cost him several games, and he finished with 94 points in 75 games. But he was back in the "century club" in 1984–85 with 105 points. In 1985–86, Savard scored a career-high 47 goals—his first of three straight seasons with at least 40 tallies.

In 1987–88, Savard reached a career high in points (131), though he continued to be overshadowed by Wayne Gretzky (whose scoring exploits put everyone else—including Savard—in Second Class Citizen status). After haggling with Chicago coach Mike Keenan for several years, Savard was traded to Montreal in 1990–91 for Norris Trophy-winning defenseman Chris Chelios. In each of his first two years in Montreal, he scored 28 goals, though his play was not up to former levels. He finally won a Stanley Cup in 1993 when Montreal ousted the Kings in the finals.

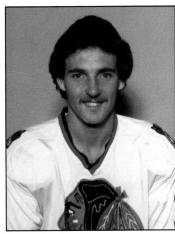

Savard holds 'Hawks team records for single-season points (131) and assists (87).

After playing the 1993–94 season with Tampa Bay, he was traded back to Chicago late in the 1994–95 season. Revitalized by his return, Savard was the 'Hawks' best player in the 1995 playoffs.

Terry Sawchuk

The argument could be made that Terry Sawchuk, who won Stanley Cups in Detroit and Toronto and captured four Vezina Trophies in a dazzling 21-year career, was the greatest goalie ever to play in the NHL. Statistically, he blazed a trail where no other netminder has dreamed of going. Sawchuk is the all-time leader in three major categories: games played by a goalie (971), shutouts (103), and career victories (435). He won 44 times in a 70-game schedule in consecutive seasons (1951 and 1952) with a .628 winning percentage. Only Bernie Parent, who won 47 in a 78-game schedule, won more games in a single season, but with a lower winning percentage (.602).

Sawchuk suffered some of the most crippling injuries imaginable: to his back, his shoulders and arms, his hands and legs—many requiring surgery. And still, he persevered, rehabilitated, bucked all the odds, and pieced together a Hall of Fame career that rivals the great performances of athletes across all sports.

Terrance Gordon Sawchuk (born December 28, 1929) began playing hockey as a child in his hometown of Winnipeg, Manitoba, and by 16

With 103 shutouts, Sawchuk is the only goalie in history to cross the century mark.

had signed a contract with the Red Wings. After winning accolades in the USHL and AHL, he went to Detroit in 1949. In his rookie season (1950–51), he replaced goalie Harry Lumley, who led the league in wins the previous season, and promptly won the Calder Trophy as rookie of the year, with 44 wins, a league-leading 11 shutouts, and a 1.99 GA average.

In his first five NHL seasons, he went 183–85–80 with a GA average under 2.00 and an amazing 56 shutouts. During that span, the Red Wings won three Stanley Cups (1952, 1954, and 1955), and Sawchuk had playoff GA averages of 0.63, 1.60, and 2.36, respectively. He also won three Vezina Trophies.

Sawchuk was traded to Boston so Detroit could make room for a youngster named Glenn Hall in 1955, but injuries stymied his career. Two years later, after a brief retirement, he was traded back to Detroit for Johnny Bucyk. The Red Wings never got back to Stanley Cup form, and in 1964, Sawchuk, then 35, was acquired by Toronto. He teamed with 40-year-old Johnny Bower, and together they shared the 1964–65 Vezina Trophy. Two years later, Sawchuk was in goal when the Maple Leafs won the Cup (1967), beating Montreal in six games.

After brief stints in L.A., Detroit, and New York, Sawchuk died suddenly in the spring of 1970 and entered the Hall of Fame in 1971.

Milt Schmidt

Without their scrappy center Milt Schmidt leading the way, it is by no means certain that the 1941 Boston Bruins would have been able to skate past Detroit to win the Stanley Cup, let alone sweep them in four games. Schmidt not only scored the game-winning goal in Game Three, he set up the game-winning goals in Games One, Two, and Four (by Pat McCreavy, Roy Conacher, and Bobby Bauer, respectively). Schmidt finished the 1941 playoff season with 11 points, atop the leader board.

Schmidt was the pivot man on the Bruins' fabled "Kraut Line," along with childhood friends Woody Dumart and Bobby Bauer (with whom he played junior

An outstanding Bruins player, coach, and GM, Schmidt's No. 15 was eventually retired.

hockey in Ontario). In a 16-year career that was sadly interrupted by the onset of World War II, Schmidt was a one-time scoring champion (1940), was once voted the game's most valuable player (1951), and won a pair of Stanley Cups (1939 and 1941).

Milton Conrad Schmidt (born March 5, 1918) was raised in Kitchener, Ontario, where he learned to skate at a young age. By his teenage years, he was playing junior hockey with Dumart and Bauer, all of whom later signed with the Bruins in the mid-1930s. By 1937–38, the trio was together again and beginning to do in the NHL what they had done in junior hockey.

In 1938–39, the Kraut Line combined for 43 goals and 92 points, and the Bruins won the regular season title in a runaway before charging on to win their first Stanley Cup in 10 years with a five-game shelling of Toronto in the Finals.

The next year, 1939–40, Schmidt led the NHL in assists (30) and points (52) and won

the Art Ross Trophy for the only time in his career. His linemates, Dumart and Bauer, finished right on his heels with 43 points apiece. Though they finished atop the regular season standings again in 1939–40, their Stanley Cup title was taken by New York. But with Schmidt at the helm, the Bruins were back on top in 1940–41, taking their third straight regular season title and reclaiming the Cup in a four-game sweep against Detroit.

Schmidt left the NHL in 1941 to enlist in the Royal Canadian Air Force, missing the next three seasons (1942–44). After a dramatic and triumphant return following WWII, Schmidt proved he still had something left when he notched 61 points in 1950–51 and was voted the game's MVP. Schmidt retired in 1955, finishing his career with 229 goals and 575 points in 778 games. He spent several seasons as a coach and GM in Boston and was elected to the Hall of Fame in 1961.

Sweeney Schriner

Though his NHL career was not especially long—lasting only 11 seasons—Sweeney Shriner left a celebrated legacy. From 1934–35, when he made his debut and was the league's top rookie, to 1945–46, when (at the age of 34) he hung up his skates, Schriner was one of the most decorated and respected players of his era.

Discovered in western Canada by New York Americans boss Red Dutton in the mid-1930s, Schriner got his NHL career off to a booming start when he blasted 18 goals and 40 points in 48 games and was awarded the Calder Trophy as the game's outstanding freshman player. Schriner immediately set about proving he was no flash in the pan by winning the NHL scoring title in each of the next two seasons. In 1935–36, he scored 19 goals and 45 points to win his first Art Ross Trophy, then added 21 goals and 46 points the following season to capture his second consecutive Ross Trophy.

David "Sweeney" Schriner (born November 30, 1911) hailed from Calgary, Alberta, where he was a natural scorer in local amateur hockey. When Red Dutton asked him to come to New York, Schriner didn't hesitate. However, after five years in New York playing second-fiddle to the more popular Rangers, the Americans began to fizzle. Prior to the 1939–40 season, Schriner was traded to the Maple Leafs for four players, including Busher Jackson, Murray Armstrong, Buzz Boll, and Doc Romnes.

In Toronto, Schriner continued to excel. In 1940–41, playing on a line with Billy Taylor and Nick Metz, he reached a new career high in goals (24), then contributed to the Leafs' Stanley Cup victory in 1941–42. That year, he scored 20 regular season goals and six more in the playoffs, including two goals in the decisive seventh game against Detroit.

Schriner teamed with Gus Bodnar and former Americans linemate Lorne Carr in 1944–45 and notched a career-high 27 goals. Though the Leafs finished a distant third to Montreal in the regular season, they played the Habs equal in the first round of playoffs, upsetting the favored Canadiens in six games. In a rematch of the 1942 finals, the Maple Leafs faced Detroit again in 1945, and Schriner got the Leafs off to a quick start by scoring the only goal in a 1–0 win in Game One. Ironically, that crucial game-winning goal would be the last playoff point of Schriner's career. Toronto held on for another seven-game series win. But after the Leafs failed to qualify for the playoffs in 1946, Schriner, with 206 goals and 410 points in 484 NHL games, retired. He earned entry to the Hall of Fame in 1962.

Eddie Shore

In many ways, Eddie Shore was to the NHL what Ty Cobb was to major league baseball: an intense, highly driven player who did things his way or not at all, and who stood on the record of his achievements, which were many, even if his friends and admirers were few.

In 1934–35, during a game between Boston and Toronto, Shore knocked the skates out from beneath Maple Leafs scoring champ Ace Bailey. The Toronto star flipped and hit his head on the ice and lay unconscious before he was rushed to the hospital, where he lay near death for several weeks. Though Bailey eventually recovered, he never played again. After an exhaustive investigation of the incident, Shore was cleared of any potential criminal charge, and Bailey even shook hands with him during an All-Star fundraiser staged in Bailey's honor.

Eddie Shore (born November 25, 1902) was raised in Saskatchewan on a wheat and cattle ranch. He wasn't a gifted player, so he applied his intense personality to the chore of practicing endlessly to become the best player he could be. He was 21 when he joined the Melville Millionaires, a Saskatchewan junior team. He later played in the Western league at Regina and Edmonton before his contract was purchased by the Bruins in 1926.

A farm-tough lad, Shore was a marvel when it came to playing through pain. His style of game often resulted in injuries—cuts, gashes, broken ribs, and the like—but he rarely missed any action, and seldom was his game noticeably diminished. In his first

Shore is the only defenseman to win the Hart Trophy four times.

NHL season (1926–27), he was second among NHL defensemen in goals (12) and was second in the league in penalty minutes (130). The following season, he led in both categories with 11 goals and 165 PIM. Shore was frequently the league's highest-scoring defenseman and among its most penalized. He was recognized—if despised in equal measure—for his brilliance with four Hart Trophies as the game's most valuable player (1933, 1935, 1936, and 1938).

In 1928–29, Shore helped the Bruins win their first Stanley Cup, beating the Rangers. The Bruins wouldn't win a second Cup for another decade. In Shore's penultimate season, 1938–39, the Bruins survived a seven-game semi-final against New York before ousting Toronto in five games. Shore had the assist on Roy Conacher's Cup-winner. Shore retired in 1940 and began a tumultuous career in management and ownership. He was elected to the Hall of Fame in 1945.

Darryl Sittler

On February 7, 1976, toward the end of the 1975–76 season, Toronto center Darryl Sittler all but ensured his place in hockey history when he single-handedly dismantled the Boston Bruins with a barrage of offensive skill never before seen in the NHL. A hard-skating playmaker with both grace and grit, Sittler scored six goals and added four assists for an unheard of 10-point game. With that sudden burst of scoring, Sittler reached the 40-goal, 100-point plateau for the first time in his career.

Darryl Glen Sittler (born September 18, 1950) grew up in Ontario and played junior hockey with the London Knights in the OHL. Selected eighth overall in the 1970 entry draft, he immediately graduated to the Maple Leafs in 1970. While he scored only modestly in his first two seasons (18 points in 1970–71 and 32 points in 1971–72), it wasn't long before Sittler was establishing himself as the team's new scoring leader. Teamed on a line with right wing sniper Lanny McDonald and left wing tough guy Dave "Tiger" Williams, the husky pivot raised his point total to 77 by his third year in the NHL, which was enough to put him at the top of the Maple Leafs' scoring chart. For the next eight years, from 1972–73 to 1979–80, Sittler reigned as the Leafs' scoring ace, twice reaching or surpassing the 100-point mark (100 points in 1975–76, 117 points in 1977–78) and four times collecting at least 40 goals.

The Leafs never won a Stanley Cup during Sittler's 12 years in Toronto and only got as far as the semis in 1977–78, when they upset the Islanders only to suffer a four-game sweep at the hands of the Stanley Cup-bound Montreal Canadiens.

It was Toronto's annual playoff failures, combined with Sittler's steadily rising salary, that resulted in his trade to Philadelphia in 1982, despite his status as Toronto's all-time leading goal-scorer (398) and point-getter (916). He proved he still had some fire with 43 goals for the Flyers in 1982–83, and 27 more in 1983–84. In January 1983, he recorded the 1,000th point of his career. But then, just as the 1984–85 season was set to begin, Sittler was sent to Detroit for a pair of youngsters. Despite his great disappointment at the trade, Sittler joined the Red Wings, played 61 games, and notched 27 points before calling it quits with 484 goals and 1,121 points in 1,096 NHL games. Though he fell short of the 500-goal mark and never won that elusive Stanley Cup, Sittler was deservedly elected to the Hall of Fame in 1988.

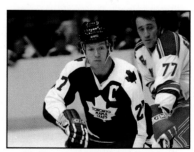

Sittler tops all Maple Leaf centers in goals, assists, points, and penalties.

gation196

Billy Smith

In the honor roll of great "money goalies" who've played in the NHL, few men hold a more distinguished place than Billy Smith, winner of four consecutive Stanley Cups with the Islanders (1980–83) and ninth among the all-time win leaders (305).

In the 1983 playoffs, when the Isles captured their fourth straight championship, Smith was at his absolute best, earning a pair of shutouts and a league-leading 2.68 goals-against average. For his excellence, Smitty was rewarded with the Conn Smythe Trophy as the post-season MVP.

William John Smith (born December 12, 1950) was born in Ontario but found his way to the Quebec junior league, where he skated for the Cornwall Royals. Originally drafted by the Los Angeles Kings in the 1970 amateur draft, Smith spent two seasons at Springfield of the American league before he was selected by the Islanders in the 1972 expansion draft. After two miserable seasons in which he won just 16 of 83 games, Smitty went 21–18–17 with a 2.78 GA average in 1974–75—the first of 12 straight winning seasons.

Though he typically shared the regular-season puckstopping workload with Glenn "Chico" Resch, Smitty was "the man" once playoffs began. During the Isles' four-year dynasty, Smith played in 72 of 78 playoff games, winning 57 while losing only 13. During that span, he established a four-year 2.63 playoff GA average. In 1982–83, he posted a 32–9–4 record and a 2.97 GA average in 46 games and won his only Vezina Trophy.

Not just a smart, intensely competitive goalie, Smitty—also known as "Battling Billy"—was a formidable tough guy. Skaters who loitered too

A tenacious netminder, Smith was in goal for four consecutive Isles Cups.

long in front of his crease were likely to feel his wrath. He frequently led all NHL goalies in penalty minutes. In 675 games with New York, he earned 13 points and 484 PIM.

On November 28, 1979, during a game against the Colorado Rockies, Smith made a save, after which a Rockies skater inadvertently shot the puck the length of the ice into his own net, which had been vacated for a delayed penalty. Smith, the last Islander to touch the puck, was credited with scoring a goal.

An 18-year NHL veteran, Smith retired in 1989 with a 305–233–105 record in 680 games and a career 3.17 GA average. His 88–36 record in 132 playoff games (with a 2.17 GAA) earned him a spot in the Hall of Fame in 1993.

Peter Stastny

The first bona fide European superstar of the NHL, Peter Stastny arrived on the NHL scene in the autumn of 1980, on the heels of being named Czechoslovakian League Player of the Year (for 1979–80). He joined the Quebec Nordiques as a 24-year-old free agent rookie and immediately set a pair of NHL records when he notched 70 assists (since broken) and 109 points. On February 22, 1981, he racked up eight points in a game against Washington (including four goals) while his linemate and kid brother, Anton, scored three goals and set up five more in the same contest. Stastny earned the Calder Trophy as the league's rookie of the year based on this brilliant debut.

Peter Stastny (born September 18, 1956) was one of three Bratislava-native Stastny brothers to skate for the Nordiques in the early 1980s. Siblings Marian and Anton each played well, but never approached the level of middle brother Peter who chalked up seven 100-point seasons in his first eight NHL years. After years of 109, 139, 124, 119, 100, and 122 points, his streak was interrupted in 1986–87 when injuries limited him to just 64 games (and 77 points). A superb playmaker, puckhandler, and skater, Stastny made his reputation as player who could set up goals with a grace that came close to matching Wayne Gretzky (who dominated the NHL during Stastny's tenure). As a sophomore in 1981–82, Stastny set up a career-high 93 goals and finished with 139 points (his best total ever). As a third-year pro in 1982–83, he pumped in 47 goals, one of five seasons in which he reached the 40-goal plateau. On October 19, 1989, "Stash" became the 24th player in NHL history to reach the 1,000-point plateau when he scored during a 5–3 win over the Blackhawks.

At the end of the 1989–90 season, after notching 380 goals and 1,048 points, the Nordiques' all-time leading scorer was traded to New Jersey for two defensemen. During the next three seasons, Stastny's once prodigious production waned. In 1993–94, he left the Devils to join his national Slovak Olympic team, scoring nine points in eight games during the 1994 Winter Games in Norway. He played parts of the 1993–94 and 1994–95 seasons with the St. Louis Blues, but his playing time was limited and his contribution was minimal.

As the 1994–95 season concluded, Stash had 450 goals in 977 NHL games in 15 NHL seasons. With 1,239 career points (giving him a 1.26 points-per-game average), the great Slovak center is perhaps the greatest European player ever to compete in the NHL.

Stastny is second all-time (behind Teemu Selanne) in rookie scoring.

Nels Stewart

It took the Montreal Maroons only four games to eliminate the Victoria Cougars from the 1926 Stanley Cup finals (taking the best-of-five series three games to one), and lanky 23-year-old rookie centerman Nels Stewart, the 1926 NHL scoring champ, netted the winning goals in each of the Maroons' three playoff victories, finishing the postseason tournament with six goals and seven points. His closest rival, teammate Babe Siebert, had just three points.

That season was one of Stewart's greatest. Despite his first-year status, he ran away with the scoring title with 34 goals and 42 points in 36 games, winning not only the Art Ross Trophy for his statistical excellence, but also taking the Hart Trophy as the league's most valuable player (his first of two). Add a Stanley Cup to the mix and the beginning of a legend was in the making.

Nels Stewart (born December 29, 1902) hailed from Montreal and developed his hockey skills in an era when local pro teams claimed first dibs on all available talent (unlike the current draft system, which disperses talent across a continent). At 23, Stewart signed up with the Montreal Maroons and made his NHL debut, establishing himself as an instant star.

Big and strong, though not flashy or graceful, Stewart was an immovable object in front of the enemy net, and he boasted a pair of soft hands when the puck reached his stick—though those same hands quickly hardened up when it came to dropping the gloves and throwing punches. As a sophomore, fol-lowing his rookie scoring title, he led the NHL in penalty minutes (133). Known as "Ol' Poison," Stewart's trailblazing style helped him become a leading goal-scorer.

In 1929–30, he reached a career-high 39 goals and 55 points and earned his second Hart Trophy as league MVP. But he could not carry the Maroons to any further postseason greatness, and in 1932, he was traded to Boston, where he spent three years. He shifted between Boston and the New York Americans twice before settling on Broadway. In 1936–37, he shared the NHL goal-scoring lead with Red Wing Larry Aurie. Following the 1939–40 season, the rambunctious forward retired.

Stewart finished his 15-year NHL career with 324 goals and 515 points—and 953 penalty minutes—in 654 games. Until Rocket Richard came along, Stewart hailed as the league's all-time leading goal-scorer. He went into the Hall of Fame in 1962.

Cyclone Taylor

A star of hockey before there was a National Hockey League, Fred Taylor's extraordinary skating artistry—his speed and lateral mobility—earned him the nickname "Cyclone" after several other monikers, among them "Tornado" and "Whirlwind," failed to tell the story adequately.

Frederick Eric Taylor (born June 23, 1883) grew up playing hockey in Ontario, long before the emergence of pro leagues that would make him a rich man in his adulthood. Always a talented stickhandler and skater, Taylor was the first player to gain fame on a steady diet of end-to-end rushes. Half a century before Bruins legend Bobby Orr "revolutionized"

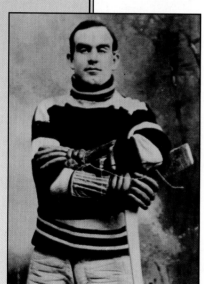

A dazzling skater, Taylor tallied 16 hat tricks—an impressive feat even today.

the NHL with his offensive brilliance, Taylor—who played both forward and defense—was turning heads with a high-speed, confident style that turned his teams into winners.

In 1908–09, he turned pro with the Ottawa Senators and helped them to an Eastern Canada Hockey Association title with a 10–2 record. By virtue of new league bylaws, Ottawa was awarded the Stanley Cup based on its ECHA title. During that rookie pro season, Taylor ripped 17 goals, a huge total for that era.

The following season (1909–10), the National Hockey Association was formed with teams in Cobalt, Haileybury, Renfrew (Ontario), and two in Montreal. Taylor signed up with Renfrew for $5,000 (making him the highest paid hockey player of his day), and thus became a hated rival among his former fans in Ottawa. Two years later, the Renfrew franchise folded, and Taylor traveled west to play in the newly formed Pacific Coast Hockey Association as a member of the Vancouver Millionaires. In 1914–15, the Millionaires challenged the NHA champion Ottawa Senators for the Stanley Cup and displayed masterful offensive strength, outscoring Ottawa 26–8 over three games to win the championship—and Taylor got his name on another Cup.

During the 1915–16 season, Taylor lived up to his nickname when he scored six goals in a game against Victoria. Then he led the PCHA in goals (32) during the 1917–18 season, despite playing in just 18 games. His Vancouver Millionaires took yet another PCHA title in 1918–19 as Taylor won yet another goal-scoring title (23).

According to one enduring legend, Taylor actually scored a goal against Ottawa (during his Renfrew days) after skating backward through the enemy, fulfilling a previous threat to embarrass his ex-mates. Taylor, who never played a game in the NHL, retired in 1923 and was inducted into the Hall of Fame in 1947.

Tiny Thompson

Had there been a trophy for rookie of the year in 1929, goaltending legend Cecil "Tiny" Thompson would have been the leading candidate to win it. Just 23 when he first skated into the Bruins' net at the start of the 1928–29 season, Thompson shook off any signs of freshman jitters, led the league in wins (26), and took Boston to a first-place finish in the American Division. In the playoffs that followed, Thompson tossed a pair of shutouts as Boston ousted powerful Montreal in the semifinals, then swept the Rangers in two games, with Thompson earning his third shutout. The Bruins raised their first-ever Stanley Cup, and their first-year goalie finished the post-season with an amazing 0.60 goals-against average in five games. Thompson was a runner-up to George Hainsworth for the Vezina Trophy with 12 regular season shutouts and a 1.18 GA average. All in his rookie season!

Cecil Thompson (born May 31, 1905) hailed from San-don, British Columbia, where he became a highly touted amateur during his late teens and early 20s. One legend claims that Bruins boss Art Ross was so impressed by reports of Thompson's play, he signed the goalie to a pro contract before he ever saw him play.

After his brilliant freshman season, Thompson proved he was the genuine article in 1929–30 when he set an NHL record (since broken) with 14 straight victories. That season, he captured the first of his four Vezina Trophies, finishing with 38 wins and the lowest GAA in the NHL (2.23).

Though the Bruins never again ascended to the Stanley Cup winners' circle during his tenure, Thompson continued to excel. In 1932–33, he led the league with 25 wins, 11 shutouts, and a 1.83 GA average, beating out Detroit's John Roach for the Vezina Trophy (his second). Three years later, he finished the 1935–36 season with a league-high 10 shutouts and a 1.71 GA average to take

his third Vezina. Two years later, at the age of 33, he led the league with 30 wins and finished the 1937–38 season with a 1.85 GA—the fourth time in 10 years he posted a sub-2.00 GA average.

Five games into the 1938–39 season, Thompson was briefly sidelined by an

In 1933, Tiny played six grueling overtime periods in a marathon battle with Toronto.

infection in one eye. After his stand-in, Frank Brimsek, proved to be masterful, Thompson was dealt to Detroit for $15,000. He finished his career in 1940 with 284 wins (15th all-time) and 81 shutouts (fifth all-time). Among goalies with at least 500 games, his 2.08 career GA is No. 1 all-time. Thompson was elected to the Hall of Fame in 1959.

Bryan Trottier

It wasn't Bryan Trottier's fault that he played most of his pro career amid the reign of Wayne Gretzky. But if there was another player in the NHL whose skill earned him "Gretzky-like" accolades, it was the Islanders' scrappy center, who guided the Isles to four Stanley Cups, then won two more Cups in Pittsburgh.

Bryan John Trottier (born July 17, 1956) was a much coveted junior during his three-year career in the Western league. Drafted by the Islanders after scoring 41 goals and 112 points in 1973–74, he left Swift Current after two years and joined Lethbridge, where he led the WHL in assists (98) in 1974–75, finishing his junior career with 103 goals and 301 points in 202 games. He went directly to the Isles in 1975–76, and his 32 goals and 95 points won him the Calder Trophy duel for rookie of the year.

In 1978–79, his fourth pro season, he won his only scoring title, capturing the Art Ross Trophy with 47 goals and 134 points. He also earned the Hart Trophy as MVP. On December 23, 1978, he set an NHL record with six points (including three goals) in one period during a 9–4 win over the Rangers. The next year, he helped the Isles win their first Stanley Cup when he led the

Trottier piloted the Islanders to a Stanley Cup dynasty in the early 1980s.

playoffs in scoring (29 points in 21 games) and won the Conn Smythe Trophy as post-season MVP. During a four-year stretch from 1980 to 1983, the Isles dominated the post-season, winning four Stanley Cups—and Trottier was typically among the point leaders.

A gritty centerman as comfortable in a checking role as he was spearheading the attack, he teamed brilliantly with Hall of Fame right winger Mike Bossy, whose goal-scoring prowess turned so many of Trottier's passes into assists.

On February 13, 1982, Trots demonstrated his own ability to put the puck in the net when he became the seventh NHLer ever to score four goals in a period during an 8–2 win over the Flyers. On January 29, 1985, he notched his 1,000th point, then, on February 13, 1990, netted his 500th career goal. A 40-goal scorer four times, Trots reached the 50-goal mark in 1981–82 and had six 100-point seasons.

In 1990–91, he left New York to join the Penguins and enjoyed two more Stanley Cups in a "seasoned veteran" role. He then took a season off to assist in coaching before playing his final season in 1993–94. The Islanders' all-time leading scorer, Trots retired with 524 goals, 901 assists, and 1,425 points in 1,279 games, placing him fifth all-time in goals and points by a center, and fourth all-time in assists by a center.

Norm Ullman

A classy center with grace, elegance, and no shortage of pure skill, Norm Ullman never won a Stanley Cup. He didn't earn a scoring title or a single MVP award. And thanks to a late-career decision to abandon the NHL for the big money of the World Hockey Association, he forfeited his chance to score 500 NHL goals, finishing 10 goals short of that prestigious plateau.

Still, he was an integral member of the Detroit Red Wings for nearly 13 years, consistently among the team's leading scorers despite playing in Gordie Howe's huge shadow. And after his trade to the Maple Leafs, he was a major contributor to Toronto's efforts for another seven seasons, often centering the team's top line.

Norman Victor Alexander Ullman (born December 26, 1935) honed his hockey skills as a youngster growing up in western Canada. At the age of 20, he traveled east to join the Stanley Cup champion Detroit Red Wings, scoring nine rookie goals and 18 points. As a sophomore, he was placed on the team's top line, with Howe and Ted Lindsay on his flanks. At the end of the 1956–57 season, Howe's 44 goals and 89 points led the league while Lindsay's 55 assists were tops. Ullman lost his spot on the top line to Alex Delvecchio the next year, but he continued to produce. Over the next seven years, Ullman averaged 24 goals and 60 points per season. Then, in 1964–65, as the team's second-line center, he led the NHL with a career-high 42 goals and was the Red Wings' top overall scorer (83 points) for the first time.

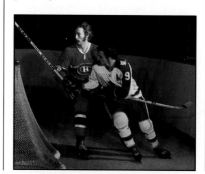

Ullman scored 20 goals 16 times in his 20 NHL seasons.

In the next three years, Detroit suffered a steady loss of their once-winning ways. Late in the 1967–68 season, Detroit and Toronto pulled off a giant seven-player trade that dealt Ullman to Toronto in exchange for Frank Mahovlich.

From 1968–69 to 1971–72, Ullman was the Leafs' top scorer. In 1970–71, he scored 34 goals and a career-high 85 points. On October 16, 1971, he notched his 1,000th point, making him the fifth man in NHL history to reach that mark. But then he missed 13 games the next year, his production fell off, and the team dropped out of playoff contention. In 1973–74, the arrival of Darryl Sittler forced Ullman to a reduced role. In 1975, he joined Edmonton and spent two years in the WHA before retiring in 1977. Detroit's fourth all-time leading scorer (758 points) and Toronto's 10th all-time leading scorer (471 points), Ullman was elected to the Hall of Fame in 1982.

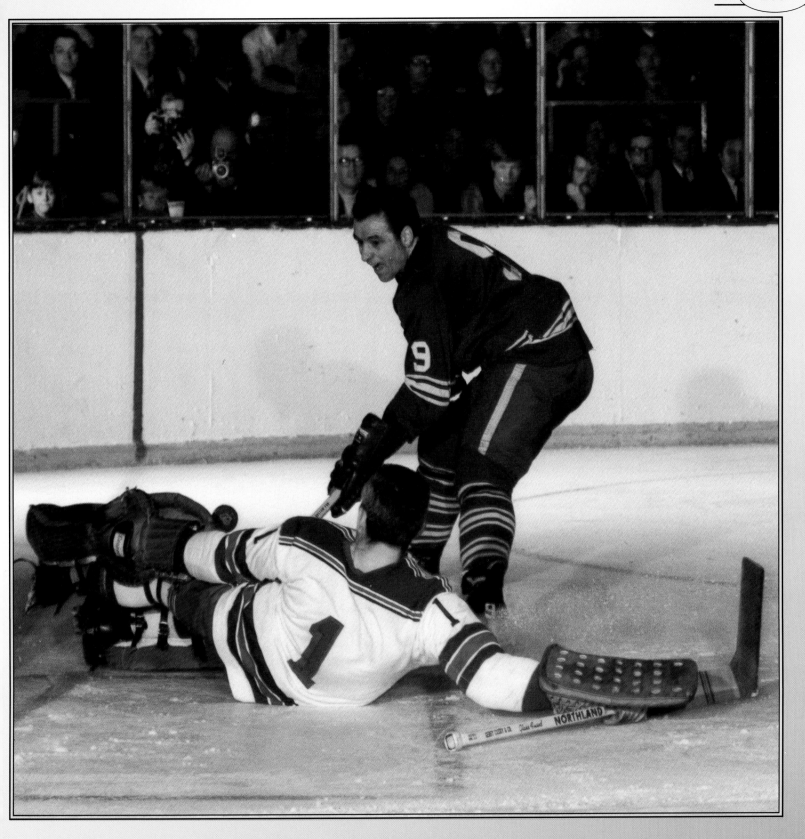

Georges Vezina

Among the more than half-dozen major awards presented to NHL players each year (Ross, Hart, Norris, Calder, Byng, Smythe, Vezina, and Selke) only one of them—the Vezina Trophy—is named after a player. All of the others honor the memories of men and women for their stature as managers, owners, and Canadian political figures. The trophy for hockey's best goalie is named for Georges Vezina, whose legendary status was forged even before the inception of the NHL and was confirmed during his eight full seasons with the Habs once they joined the league. Just one year after Vezina's untimely death at the age of 39, the NHL

Vezina never missed one game throughout his decorated 15-year career.

presented the first annual Vezina Trophy to George Hainsworth, the Habs next great goalie.

Georges Vezina (born in January of 1887) was happy in his status as a local hero tending goal for an amateur club in his native Chicoutimi, Quebec (often playing without skates, according to some legends), when, in his 23rd year, he was discovered by the Montreal Canadiens. The Habs had traveled to Vezina's hometown for an exhibition and went away losers, shut out by the man known as the "Chicoutimi Cucumber" for his cool demeanor. Vezina was immediately recruited by and became a member of the Canadiens, beginning a pro career that would stretch over 16 seasons. In 1915–16, the Habs won their first Stanley Cup, with Vezina in goal, beating Portland of the PCHA.

In 1917–18, Vezina played his first NHL season and led all goalies with 13 wins and a 3.93 GA average. The following season, though he was overshad-

owed in the regular season by Ottawa's Clint Benedict, he took the Habs back to the Cup finals, which were suspended after a flu epidemic took the life of Canadien Joe Hall.

Montreal failed to qualify for the playoffs from 1919 to 1923, but in 1923–24, Vezina once more ascended to greatness with a 2.00 GA average. He then held Calgary to just one goal over two games in the Stanley Cup finals, sweeping the series.

His last NHL season (1924–25) was in many ways his best. He posted a 1.87 GA average in the regular season, then played bravely in a losing effort against Victoria in the Stanley Cup finals, though he was already in the grips of tuberculosis. He dressed for the season opener in 1925–26, but collapsed midway through the game and was rushed to the hospital, his career over. Less than a year later, he was dead. For his excellence, he was honored with a trophy in his name and elected to the Hall of Fame in 1945.

Gump Worsley

On May 1, 1965, the Canadiens and Blackhawks were set to do battle in Game Seven of the 1965 Stanley Cup finals when Habs coach Toe Blake notified Gump Worsley, his tubby 36-year-old second-string goalie, that he was going to start. Without a doubt, it was the biggest game in Worsley's career, and it gave him a chance to redeem himself after years of misery with the Rangers. To help things along, Montreal's ace center Jean Beliveau scored 14 seconds into the game, but it was Worsley who was the real hero. He held off the powerful 'Hawks offense, recording a 4–0 Cup-winning shutout.

For Worsley, it was a long climb back to celebrity. A dozen years earlier, he was the NHL's top rookie, winner of the 1953 Calder Trophy, after playing 50 games and earning a 3.06 GA average for the 17–37–16 last-place Rangers, taking over for longtime goalie hero Chuck Rayner. After winning rookie glory, however, Gump didn't even make the Rangers squad in 1953–54, sent back to the minors in favor of newly acquired Johnny Bower. Back for the 1954–55 season, Worsley spent the next nine years on a Rangers team that failed to qualify for the playoffs five times and was eliminated in the opening round the other four. He paid rich dues, leading the NHL in losses four times during his Rangers tenure. No wonder he called his departure from NYC as the day he "got out of the Ranger jailhouse."

Lorne John Worsley (born May 14, 1929) was raised in Montreal, where his childhood mates nicknamed him for his resemblance to cartoon character Andy Gump. He played junior hockey with the Verdun Cyclones, where he caught the eye of Rangers scouts who invited him to training camp when he was 20. For the next three years, Worsley climbed steadily through the minor league ranks until he debuted with the Rangers in 1952–53 and earned rave rookie reviews. In 10 seasons with New York, the pudgy goalie played 583 games with a 204–271–101 record and a 3.10 GA average.

Once he got home to Montreal, Worsley's fortunes improved markedly. Regular participants in the Stanley Cup playoffs, the Habs won three Cups with Worsley in goal (1965, 1966, and 1968) and another with him backing Rogie Vachon (1969). Gump won 92 of 172 games and shared two Vezina Trophies (1966 and 1968).

In 1970, he was sold to Minnesota, where he finished his career with a 335–353–150 record and a 2.90 GA average in 862 games. One of the last goalies to play without a mask, Worsley was elected to the Hall of Fame in 1980.

Fearless in the face of flying pucks, Worsley was afraid to travel by plane.

Steve Yzerman

It took Steve Yzerman 12 years to realize a professional dream of playing in the Stanley Cup finals, which his Detroit Red Wings accomplished in the spring of 1995. But Yzerman's hopes of capturing a playoff championship were dashed when the New Jersey Devils swept Yzerman and the high-scoring Red Wings in the finals.

Known for many years in Detroit as "Stevie Wonder" for his brilliant skating, his artistry with the puck, and his ability to find openings in the armor of goalies that other players failed to perceive, Yzerman scored at least 50 goals three times and twice finished with more than 60 tallies. His string of 100-point seasons was halted at six when injuries limited him to 58 games and 82 points in 1993–94.

Steve Yzerman (born May 9, 1965) started life in western Canada but traveled east to play his junior hockey in the Ontario league, spending two years at Peterborough. After a modest 64-point rookie year, he erupted with 91 points in 56 games as a 17-year-old in 1982–83, and, based on the acclaim his performance gained him, he was the fourth player chosen in the 1983 entry draft.

In 1983–84, Yzerman immediately proved he was ready for prime time when he collected 39 goals and 87 points in 80 games, earning a place on the All-Rookie team. After a 30-goal, 89-point sophomore campaign, Yzerman's career took a brief nosedive when a knee injury ruined his 1985–86 season, and he returned with just 31 goals and 90 points in 1986–87. Though these numbers would have been considered excellent for the majority of NHLers, for Yzerman they weren't good enough.

However, the newly named team captain persevered, working extra hard to live up to the "C" on his jersey, and in 1987–88 his efforts paid off. For the first time in his career, Yzerman scored 50 goals and 102 points and launched himself into legitimate stardom. He followed up in 1988–89 with a career-high 65 goals and 155 points, earning the Lester B. Pearson Award as the players' choice for MVP. In 1989–90, Yzerman ripped another 62 goals and 127 points, though the Red Wings failed to qualify for the playoffs for the second time in his tenure. After a 51-goal display in 1990–91, the flashy centerman dropped to 45 the following year before again reaching the 50-goal plateau in 1992–93 (58).

When the 1994–95 season concluded, Yzerman, a 12-year veteran, had 481 goals and 1,160 points to his credit in 862 games, giving him the fifth-highest points-per-game average all-time (1.345).

Yzerman is one of only four NHL players to score 150 points in a season.